FAILURE
TO
COMPLY

FAILURE
TO
COMPLY

WE FOUGHT A WALL STREET GIANT AND WON

Terry Puffer Ray & Allen Ray

To order additional copies of this book, contact:
Xlibris LLC
1-888-795-4274
www.Xlibris.com
Orders@Xlibris.com
110312

CONTENTS

Since the securitization process allows for more profit—the more predatory (and, therefore, illegal) the loan is, there is an inherent incentive to violate the borrowers' rights during the origination and servicing processes.

—Ohio attorney Daniel L. McGookey

CHAPTER 1

A Nuclear Accident

IT WAS THE sound of something about to happen, a low rhythmic warning growl. A sixty-five-thousand-pound semitruck going sixty-five miles per hour hit the freeway rumble strip as a warning that the truck was moving too close to the side of the road. Allen, my husband of thirty-two years, was on the side of the road trying to fix a flat tire on the company car he was driving. He was on his way to Toledo, Ohio, with a delivery of nuclear medicine when the tire on his car blew out. He had pulled over onto the berm of the freeway to assess the damage and check on the nuclear syringes contained within heavy lead cases. It was July 10, 2007—a day that would be hard to forget. July 10, 2007, was also the day that Standard & Poor's announced that "it would shortly downgrade its credit ratings on billions of dollars worth of mortgage-backed securities," according to David Faber, author of *And Then the Roof Caved In*. These two unlikely events on the very same day would forever become intertwined for us and change our lives forever.

He was getting back into the small company car to get to his cell phone when there was the sound of a bomb exploding! The semitruck had hit him and his car. The door and the windshield exploded, sending thousands of pieces of glass into the air. Suddenly, he felt extreme pain and was not exactly sure what happened. The door of the car was ripped right out of his hand and was bent forward upon the impact of the semitruck hitting the small car. He was in shock, and adrenaline began pumping throughout his body. The adrenaline rush allowed him to go into autopilot, and his next concern was checking on the nuclear cargo. Any incident involving nuclear material is a very serious matter to the state and federal government, especially along an interstate. The syringes were still contained and he had avoided a nuclear incident, but that day set in motion several serious events in our personal and financial lives. It began when I got the telephone call no wife wants to receive.

I was working as a senior title examiner and production team lead for the second largest title company in the United States. The day had been very hectic, as always, as I was working with title reports being produced by teams in India and the Philippines for banks in the United States trying to modify borrowers' home loans. In worse case scenarios, the borrowers were heading into mortgage foreclosure, so those reports had to be accurate and truthful as to what was happening with their titles. There were laws that needed to be followed if a property was foreclosed, and these reports were being used by foreclosure lawyers. The liability for my title insurance company and the law firms they were serving was great if something was missed by these inexperienced teams overseas.

"Honey, can you come get me? I am on Ohio Interstate 80 and have just been hit by a semitruck. I am hurt pretty bad, but I am alive," my husband said on the phone call.

I was shocked by his call, and adrenaline started coursing throughout my body! I had to keep it together and get into my car and get to my husband and bring him home.

I just started driving on the interstate when my cell phone rang again. It was Allen, and he informed me that his company was sending another courier to pick up the nuclear medicine and that the courier would bring him home. I wanted him to go to the nearest hospital, but he insisted he wanted to come home first. He said, "Terry, if I am going to die today, then I would rather be as close to home as possible."

I couldn't imagine the kind of pain he was feeling at that moment for him to have said this to me.

The injuries Allen sustained were severe to his left hand, left arm, back, neck, and hip. The cuts sustained from the shards of glass hitting him in the face and head eventually healed, and the fact that he wore glasses probably saved his eyesight. But he would spend over two years in and out of the hospital trying to heal his hand and arm. You don't realize how miraculous the hand and fingers are until you cannot use them for everyday tasks. But he never gave up and followed the doctor's instructions and the physical therapists' advice at Metro General Hospital in Cleveland for the next two years.

While he was out of work, our budget began to really tighten. We were now living off one income. Before the accident, Allen had been working two full-time jobs. He delivered the nuclear medicine from

TERRY PUFFER RAY & ALLEN RAY

midnight to 8:00 a.m., and then he would go to work as a title examiner from 9:00 to 5:00. We did what every middle-class family does in times of financial trouble—we cut back on everything. We grocery-shopped at Aldi and Save-A-Lot. We bought basic necessities at Family Dollar stores. We cut out all premium television channels and went to basic cable. When winter came, we set the thermostat to sixty degrees and kept it there to avoid high heating bills. By the end of 2007, we knew that Allen's rehabilitation would take almost two years. That meant our budget would continue to tighten severely.

The home we lived in at the time of Allen's accident was going to be the home we fixed up to sell one day for a little profit, and that money would be used for our retirement. We had about ten years till that day, so we had the time to do some updating. It was a beautiful home built in the 1950s. Our backyard was nestled against the trees of the Cleveland Metroparks and provided complete privacy. Our living room window was the size of a normal wall—overlooking the trees, shrubs, and even the beautiful wild deer of the park. It was our dream home, and this view of the outdoors reminded me of homes built by the famous architect Frank Lloyd Wright. He was fond of the concept of bringing the outdoors visually into an indoor living space. This was our Frank Lloyd Wright—style home, and we would have done anything to keep our home.

We bought this home in 2002 with a 20 percent down payment and, in 2005, refinanced our loan to make further improvements as planned. We didn't take all the money we could have on home refinance and left 20 percent equity in the home. This was not typical for the time. Many homeowners in our situation were taking out all the equity in their homes or borrowing money with interest-only loans. The most exotic we got with our financing was to borrow the money with an adjustable-rate mortgage. It offered a low introductory interest rate that would reset one year later. Our plan was to refinance within two to three years into a fixed-rate mortgage.

"The best-laid plans of mice and men often go awry."

Allen had been hit in July 2007, and by the end of that year, as we predicted, we could not keep up with our adjustable-rate mortgage, and our savings were almost gone. We called the bank to let them know our particular situation and to see if we could work something out. After all, I worked for the second largest title insurance company and saw title reports for thousands of loan modifications every week with some of the biggest banks in the country, including our bank. Borrowers were obtaining loan modifications all the time, so how hard could it be? Allen called our bank to inquire about a loan modification.

The servicer of the loan was Citi-Residential. They took Allen's call and seemed receptive to a loan mod. They asked us to fill out an application and fax it to them, which we did immediately. We were trying to be proactive in this difficult financial period in our lives and thought if Citi-Residential was willing to work with us, we would cooperate to the fullest. But after faxing the application to them, days and then weeks went by with no communication. We tried calling them, and the answer was "We lost your application, Mr. and Mrs. Ray. Would you send it again to us?" We said we would, as we knew that faxes can get lost in the shuffle. Again, it was days and weeks that no word came from Citi-Residential. So we called once again. They apologized for not getting back to us and said again that they had lost our paperwork. Would we mind sending it to them *again*?

We became increasingly concerned because it was now the beginning of 2008 and this servicer kept losing our paperwork. Our savings were almost gone now. It had been a very cold winter, and the bills kept adding up as we tried to stay warm in our home.

It was June of 2008, and months and months had gone by trying to get a loan modification application reviewed by the bank. We were now out of savings, and Allen called the bank to let them know we would not be able to make our house payment next month. After almost a year of trying to work with them on a loan modification application, they told him that they would not be able to modify our loan until we were two months behind on our payments! We had been talking to them for months, and this was the first time we had ever heard that! We had to be two months behind in payments to get a loan mod? We had never heard of such a thing. Wasn't that the purpose of a loan modification—so the borrower would not become delinquent on their payments? We now felt as if we had been strung along by the bank. Why would the bank not want its money from us under a loan modification? It didn't make sense.

When the housing market crashed in September of 2008, it became clear to us why we had been stonewalled for over a year. But in the interim, once the housing bubble burst, so did all the home values. Our one option to get out from underneath our personal financial crisis would have been to sell our home and move on with our lives. But the 2008 collapse left our home devalued by almost $60,000—which meant we now owed more on the loan than what the house was worth.

Desperately, we tried to find a solution to the problem that we faced. It had now been two months since we were unable to make our house payment, so perhaps now the bank's servicer, Citi-Residential, would modify our mortgage. We called one more time to see if we could come together on a solution. Their response was unexpected. They said they were sorry about Allen's truck accident, but there was nothing they could do for us. We explained that they had said they would accept our loan modification application if we were two months behind. We were now behind the required amount of time, so we asked if we could proceed. There was silence on the other end of the phone call and a click. The call had been ended.

In November of 2008, instead of getting loan modification papers in the mail to sign, we got legal papers delivered to our house by a deputy of the Common Pleas Court of Cuyahoga County. We were being sued for foreclosure by a bank we hadn't even heard of in conjunction with our home loan! The plaintiff's name on the lawsuit was ███████████ ██████████████████████████ as trustee, in trust for the registered holders of Ameriquest Mortgage Securities Inc., Asset-Backed Pass-Through Certificates, Series 2005-R6.

We had signed an old-fashioned mortgage refinance in 2005 with Ameriquest Mortgage Company, which was being serviced by Citi-Residential and with whom we had spent a year working to modify our loan, and now a bank named █████████████████████ was suing us for foreclosure! It was as if a nuclear bomb exploded in our lives, and the ripples of yet unseen consequences would radiate out and impact us for the next year.

CHAPTER 2

We Will Crush You

WHEN WE PURCHASED our home in Berea, Ohio, in 2002 and refinanced in 2005, we thought we were signing an old-fashioned mortgage. We never expected that our home and mortgages would become a part of a securitized transaction on Wall Street. We had been working with mortgages for years as a part of our work as title examiners. We had seen mortgages written in the 1940s through the 2000s. The mortgages from the '40s were two, maybe three, pages in length at most. Then in the 1990s and 2000s, mortgages were thirty to forty pages long. Who could read and understand that many pages of legal lingo on a home mortgage? What had changed in fifty years to home mortgages that so many pages were now required?

Mortgage-backed securities (or securitization for short) are what happened. Traditional community banks were no longer the only ones involved in selling you a mortgage. Nontraditional banks, which we like to call pretender lenders, were now in the game. These banks did not even have minimum cash reserves on hand and were writing trillions of dollars worth of loans with minimum oversight.

In 1989, we purchased our very first home in Lakewood, Ohio. This mortgage was not securitized, and we were never late on any of our payments for this house. It was a beautiful 1911 colonial house with the kind of porch that said "come on over and sit awhile." A porch in those days was a retreat from the summer heat long before air conditioning was created. Ours was no different—decorated with wicker chairs, a sofa, and a hundred-year-old Victorian wicker plant stand proudly displaying a huge green Boston fern.

We improved this home ourselves, putting up new cherry kitchen cabinets, countertops, and new appliances. We wanted a deck off the back of our home and found a true craftsman named Lou Schubert who built us the most elegant deck. He came to stay with us one evening and slept in our spare room. He didn't leave for three years after that first night.

But during those three years, he improved our home and garden and told us wonderful stories about his days growing up in New York City. Lou used to pal around with Jackie Robinson Jr. in New York in the late 1950s and the early 1960s. Jackie Sr. was the famous baseball player. Lou and Jackie Jr. would bop around town in a bright red Thunderbird convertible, going to jazz clubs to listen to the great jazz players of the time like Miles Davis and John Coltrane. We loved Lou's stories, and we loved his carpentry work and gardening talent.

We had old-fashioned roses that were so fragrant and colorful in the summer heat, a purple lilac bush that gave off its fragrance in the spring, miniature maple trees, shrubs, water fountains, and evening lights showing it all off when the sun went down. People who came to visit us used to say our garden was a "Mr. Miyagi" garden right out of the movie *Karate Kid*.

After three years, we put the 1911 colonial up for sale. This was right about the time of the real estate bubble, when even average houses were going up in value every year. With all the work Lou did to help us improve our home and the money we spent in improvements, we got a price well over the comps for the neighborhood.

I had been shopping around for another home with more trees and more privacy than the colonial provided in Lakewood. This was a Cleveland suburb with more houses per square mile than any other suburb around. I scoured the newspaper's real estate sections regularly and found the house that Allen and I would live in forever. We took our money and bought our 1950s Berea Cape Cod house that had the Cleveland Metroparks as our backyard.

Little did we know that a few years after living in our new home, Allen would be hit by a semitruck. Allen began what turned out to be two years of healing and rehabilitation. How fortunate we are that he survived the impact of the sixty-five-thousand-pound truck! He had a second chance at life and was determined to make the most of it.

To deal with the pain of his treatments and the eventual boredom of endless hand and arm exercises, he began learning about the financial crisis affecting the housing industry in our country. He had been an excellent title examiner for years before adding a second full-time career in nuclear medicine, where he delivered nuclear syringes around the state to cancer patients. Allen has one of those intellects that is always curious about learning something new. So he did what he knew best—he began researching this crisis.

I continued to work full time to keep us afloat, and Allen healed his body and researched. I was the beneficiary of all his knowledge and research about the securitization of millions and millions of home mortgages between 1997 and 2008. He was the beneficiary of my work as a senior title examiner for the second largest title insurance company in the United States. He would read about all the home mortgages going into securitized trusts to be sold to investors, and I was seeing, in real application, those mortgage trusts on the documents I was reviewing for our title reports and insurance policies. Together, we got smarter and stronger as a team with one goal in mind: to save our home.

One of my early duties when I began working at this title insurance company in 2005 was to type up hundreds of title policies. Between 2005 and 2008, there were thousands of policies created for lenders, such as Wells Fargo Bank, Chase, Citibank, and Ameriquest. They all had funny long names, I thought at the time—like Wells Fargo Bank as trustee for the Asset-Backed Trust 2006-OPT2 Mortgage Pass-Through Certificates, Series 2006-2. I had no idea that these were the mortgage-backed securities being packaged on Wall Street to be sold to investors as AAA-rated investments. These were the very securities that created the financial crisis of 2008.

We learned that between 1997 and 2007, securitization tripled the amount of mortgage-backed securities to $7.3 trillion in the United States. There was very little regulatory oversight by the Federal Reserve, which was supposed to be the super regulator as spelled out in the Financial Services Modernization Act of 1999. Can you imagine any other industry in America that sold trillions of dollars worth of goods or services to consumers in this country without regulation? Think of the thousands of home appliances sold that you have to plug into an electrical outlet. What if there was no regulatory oversight by the UL (Underwriters Laboratory)? Thousands of us could possibly get shocked when we plugged in our toaster or coffeemaker. Yet Wall Street was selling $7.3 trillion worth of securities, backed by or secured by our homes with little regulation! The middle class in this country as a consumer of these securitized mortgages were not notified that their homes were being put at risk with these mortgage-backed securities. These borrowers thought they were signing an old-fashioned mortgage or an old-fashioned refinance—not a securitized investment scheme.

So what happens to all that paperwork for trillions of dollars of mortgages? Who holds on to the original documents, the note, and the mortgage? After all, history shows that these documents are critically important if there is a default on the loan. How would a lender prove that he was the owner of your loan and had been harmed by you not paying back your debt? Without the original note and mortgage in the rightful hands of the owner of the loan, anyone could step forward and say that you owed them the money.

What happens during securitization is that the original notes and mortgages are merely tossed aside or even shredded, like a head of cabbage for coleslaw. The note is the document that evidences the debt on your home. The mortgage is the document that spells out the terms of your loan, the interest rate, the length of time, and what happens if you default on the note. After you sign the mortgage, it is recorded in the county recorder's office in your state where you reside. It is now considered a public record and visible for all to see.

The note is handled differently. It is delivered, acknowledged, and endorsed by the bank—who now owns your loan. Normally, it is not recorded in the county records, but the original note is very important, nonetheless, and would be kept in a safe place within the bank in case you should go into default and into foreclosure. The bank would need to produce this note and show it to the court to prove they are the owner and holder of your note and have the legal capacity to foreclose on you and take away your home.

During the lead-up to the housing crash of 2008, millions of loans were being written in this country. Those of us who worked in the title industry assumed that the mortgages and notes were being handled as they always had been. Homes and property have been conveyed for hundreds of years, and proofs of those conveyances from our time to those one hundred years ago and older are kept in your local county recorder's office. The really old deeds are usually in a special room and found in old leather-bound books that smell of age. The deeds are yellowed now, and the handwriting, done with quill pen and ink, tells of a time long past.

At the beginning of the housing crisis of 2008, many people who were smarter than I began speaking out about the crisis on evening news on channels like MSNBC, CNN, or *60 Minutes*. When you are facing foreclosure, as we were, pay attention to everything around you; it is amazing what you can discover.

One evening, a United States congresswoman from Ohio named Marcy Kaptur was on the Lou Dobbs program. She was talking about the foreclosure crisis in this country. My ears immediately perked up, and I listened intently. She was the first person to teach me about how Wall Street bundled all these mortgage loans together for investments. They put them into a real estate mortgage investment conduit for tax-avoidance purposes. The conduit was to remain intact, and mortgages could not be moved once they were a part of the REMIC, or else there would be IRS consequences. The investment banks could owe the federal government millions and millions of dollars in tax revenues if the Real Estate Mortgage Investment Conduit's rules were violated.

She went on to say that the originals were "shredded like cabbage into coleslaw," and for a bank to prove they were the owner and holder of the note, it would be like turning "coleslaw back into the head of cabbage." She advised anyone facing foreclosure to stay in their homes and find a lawyer who understood mortgage securitization and fight to save your home.

Congresswoman Kaptur inspired me that evening to stay and fight for my home. I shared with Allen what I had learned that night, and he agreed to join me in the fight!

The next time Citi-Residential, the lender's servicer, called us about our loan, we tried on our newfound knowledge. We had nothing to lose and everything to gain. We took a deep breath and stated, "Would you please validate this debt by providing us with the original note and mortgage?"

There was a long pause on the other end of the line. They said, "Would you hold on, Mr. Ray?"

We agreed and held our breath, wondering what was coming next.

They came back on the line and said, "We don't need to do that. And who do you think you are asking us to validate the debt? We will not do this, but what we will do is destroy your credit so you and your wife will never be able to buy another home in your lifetime. We will destroy you to the point that you will have difficulty finding a job in the future because your credit will be so bad."

Their next words to us will never be forgotten as long as we live. They said, "Mr. and Mrs. Ray, don't you know how big a bank we are? We will *crush you* in a court of law! Good-bye!"

CHAPTER 3

Change Coleslaw Back into Cabbage?

E VEN A BANK worth $2.742 trillion can't change coleslaw back into cabbage once it is shredded. All the money in the world can't do that. If you don't have the original note and mortgage, you cannot prove you have the right to take someone's home! But when a bank as large as ███████████████ tells you they are going to crush you, the adrenaline starts pumping. All your senses are heightened, and you begin listening to experts all around you. We began reading everything on the subject, and we called on all our experiences as title examiners. Suddenly, everything to do with fighting a mortgage foreclosure was within our view.

██

██████████ As stated, in terms of total worldwide assets, it is worth $2,742,000,000,000. Going up against a bank with this much money would be a huge task. We were down to one regular paycheck, and our savings were depleted trying to stay current on our mortgage as a result from Allen's truck accident. Our income to fight this battle was miniscule compared to the money available in their coffers.

Where do you begin such a defense? Research. My husband loved to research, so we formulated a game plan. He would use the time he had during his physical rehabilitation to learn as much as he could about the mortgage meltdown and how it applied to our situation.

He learned about credit derivatives, CDOs (or collateralized debt obligations), third-party payouts, securitization chains of ownership, and ████████████████. How did each of these foreign-sounding things impact us here in Ohio and our old-fashioned mortgage?

I grew up in a small town in Ashtabula, Ohio, in which some of my closest friends were of Jewish descent. They would invite me to temple services whenever a rabbi would come to town. Our town was so small, and the number of Jews who lived in Ashtabula was so limited that a full-time Rabbi could not be supported. But sometimes on those days when a rabbi traveled from Cleveland, I would be invited to the temple. My friends embraced me as if I were family.

During our times together, they would share their very personal stories about growing up in Germany before and during the war. Max Freilich and his brother Felix lost their parents in a concentration camp. Max was fortunate enough to study tool and die making in Germany, a trade he practiced at a company named True Temper when he came to the United States. His brother Felix would tell stories of how he took the train every day to music school to study the violin. Felix Freilich was so talented at the violin that when he came to America, he auditioned to the Cleveland Orchestra and was accepted. He played many years with the Cleveland Orchestra, one of the premiere orchestras in the world. I was fortunate enough to go see him play on many occasions. Although, always in the back of my mind was the tragedy of the holocaust and what these two brothers and their families had suffered.

Max and his wife, Anita, had two children, Miriam and David. They were my friends in high school. Miriam and David grew up without grandparents as a result of the holocaust. But the family unit was so strong that both were extremely successful people in their own right. Miriam was an outstanding concert pianist, who often accompanied me singing or playing a Mozart flute concerto. Miriam could have played in Carnegie Hall or Severance Hall but chose to go into the healing arts as a nurse graduate of Case Western Reserve. David became a successful corporate lawyer with Volvo Car Corporation in New York.

It occurred to me that ████████████, along with seven other banks, had a cruel history of removing people from their homes. Was this the opponent we were facing? The same one who helped finance concentration camps and used people as slave laborers for their benefit? Was ████████████ the same business entity that played a role in the devastation of my friends' family? Wasn't it the Spanish philosopher and essayist George Santayana who said, "Those who cannot remember the past are condemned to repeat it"? I was determined to remember the past, and I vowed not to allow ████████████ to remove me from my home, as they did my friends. I would fight to protect my family and to remember six million other families who were taken from their homes seventy years ago.

Now that we knew the history of our opponent, we needed to find out what they were doing to the average American homeowner. What were the inventions like credit default swaps and collateralized debt obligations? A credit default swap is a type of insurance. It is an insurance an investor can buy to protect themselves against financial loss if their investment in a collateralized debt obligation goes bad. So if you defaulted on your home mortgage, they would actually make money with the credit default swaps they purchased.

What is a CDO (collateralized debt obligation)? It is a type of investment package made up of debt obligations or debt instruments. Wall Street packaged and sold our credit card debt obligations or maybe our automobile debt obligations or, most certainly, our home mortgage debt obligations to investors. This means they bundled together a group of promissory notes secured by our mortgage payments and sold those bundles to investors called certificate holders. A bundle usually contained five thousand promissory notes, mortgages, and assignments. The bundle was then given a fancy long name and put into trusts, like the Ameriquest Mortgage Securities Inc., Asset-Backed Pass-Through Certificates, Series 2005-R6.

In the old days, the banker would keep the notes and mortgages in a bank vault for protection. These original documents were very important in case there was a default. The bank wanted to be sure they could provide the court with the originals to prove they were the owner and holder of the note and the mortgage and had the legal right to sue you for foreclosure.

But with securitization of millions of home loans between 1997 and 2008, the banks we call pretender lenders got sloppy with the originals. In our opinion, we think many of these pretender lenders just threw away the originals. They put down on an accounting sheet just your name, home address, loan number, the amount owed, and the terms of the mortgage. This was much easier than holding on to millions of pieces of paper. Originals could get lost and custodians of the documents might not treat them with the kind of care your old-fashioned banker would have by putting them into a bank vault.

But what would happen if you went into foreclosure because you were unable to make your payments on a timely basis? How could pretender lenders legally sue you if they didn't have the originals? Their solution to the problem was to fraudulently recreate your note and mortgage using companies like DOCX, a subsidiary of Lender Processing Services. These companies would recreate not only your note and mortgage, but also assignments, lost note affidavits, and even entire origination files for lenders who may have lost them.

The problem that arises with creating assignments is that the laws of foreclosure are ignored. You cannot foreclose on a homeowner in our state, Ohio, and many others if you have not been assigned the mortgage. You cannot foreclose on someone just because you want to do so.

Think of it this way. It is like the three legs holding up a stool. One leg of the stool represents the bank's legal standing to sue you; the second leg represents the bank's legal capacity to sue you, and the third leg must show proof that the bank has been harmed financially. All three of these legs must be present in order for the seat to be held up. The seat is the bank's legal right to foreclose your mortgage.

Many of these Wall Street investment banks, including our own, have tried taking our homes from us without having a solid foundation in the law to do so. This includes our own lender who filed foreclosure against us before they were even the assignee of record. Then to add insult to injury, they were only the trust filing legal suit against us. They were not the original creditor who put up the money for our loan. Ameriquest Mortgage Company would be the only one who could sue us for foreclosure. But by November 2008, when we received our foreclosure papers, Ameriquest was closed for business, and no other bank was correctly assigned our note and mortgage.

The most important issue for you to remember if you are facing mortgage foreclosure is that even the creditor or investor who put up the money for your loan may not have been harmed by you defaulting on your home loan because of the credit default swaps purchased. These are known as third-party payouts. You need to insist on seeing your accounting spreadsheet to determine if your mortgage was paid for with any third-party payout money. There may be no money owed anymore on your loan, and you definitely have a right to know that.

CHAPTER 4

What They Don't Want You to Know about Third-Party Payouts

EVER WONDER WHY American International Group (AIG) received over $85 billion from the federal government in the TARP (Troubled Asset Relief Program)? AIG was one of the insurance companies being used by the Wall Street investment banks for all the credit default swaps. The bankers on Wall Street knew that many of the mortgage-backed security bundles of promissory notes and mortgages were toxic, but they were allowed to purchase insurance against that toxicity. I remember watching several CEOs of these investment banks testify before a congressional hearing in 2009. They admitted that they were aware that many of the packages were, in their words, crap. But the ratings agencies like Standard & Poor's, Moody's, and Fitch gave those mortgage-backed securities a AAA rating! Moreover, AIG was selling the investment banks credit default swaps, so why not sell those bundles of toxic "crap" to unsuspecting investors? The Wall Street banks could not lose.

In our research, we learned how insidious the credit default swaps market became during this time. One of our great teachers was a man named Neal Garfield, an outstanding lawyer with experience in securitization and author of the blog *Living Lies*. He is one of those rare individuals, who, in my opinion, can take a complicated subject like the derivatives market of which credit default swaps are a part and make it clear enough for those of us not working on Wall Street to understand. He is joined in this mission to make this information understandable by Brad Kaiser, a former employee of Fifth Third Bank of Cincinnati, Ohio. Brad was the head of sales for Fifth Third Bank, and during his tenure there, revenues went from $20 million to $600 million. Brad and Neal have an excellent background in foreclosure defense and forensic review. They have the knowledge of how Wall Street securitized and sold these Ponzi schemes called mortgage-backed securities to hedge funds, pension funds, mutual funds, and even sovereign wealth funds.

Home loans were bundled with as many as five thousand others and sold into a pool as a securitization investment. The pretender lenders (a term Neal uses to describe investment banks on Wall Street and not your local federally regulated community bank) bought credit default swaps on some of the nonperforming mortgages in the investment pool. Remember that this is a type of insurance policy used to protect Wall Street if you default on your mortgage. As Neal describes it, this insurance is like a homeowner's policy that protects you against fire. Let's say the policy will not pay you the full value of your home if you have a fire within the first year of the insurance policy. If you were dishonest, you might have fire on the 366th day in order to collect the full value of your home.

Wall Street did just that with the insurance they bought on the mortgage-backed securities. They knew that many of these loans would fail on a certain date and bought insurance accordingly. They deliberately built failure into the system in order to collect trillions of dollars in credit default swaps. If you couldn't make your new house payment when your adjustable-rate mortgage interest rate changed, raising your payment another $500 a month, for example, they didn't care. They were making even more money when you couldn't pay!

Because there was very little regulation or oversight of the derivatives markets on Wall Street, they were allowed to purchase multiple insurance policies on your home loan. Can you imagine in the example we just discussed if you were able to purchase thirty fire insurance policies for your home? That would mean that when your house burned down on the 366th day, you would have been able to collect thirty times the full value of your home! That is exactly what Wall Street did on your home loan. When you defaulted on your loan, they made as much as thirty times the value of your original loan!

The derivatives market is so complicated and so secretive that some financial groups estimate that Wall Street could have purchased more than thirty policies. Allen and I have read that the number could be as high as one hundred. For illustration, let's say thirty was the number purchased for your loan. You may have borrowed $200,000. So 30 times $200,000 equals $6 million. Now do you see why they don't want you to know about third-party payouts? Now do you understand why the investment bank didn't want to modify your loan? They would only make money if you defaulted on your mortgage!

What has bothered me the most in all this financial chaos created by the greed of Wall Street is the deflection of blame on the middle class. We are being told in the media that we were the greedy ones scamming the lenders and this housing crisis was our fault. The middle class may be guilty of signing what they thought were old-fashioned mortgages. We may be guilty of not understanding all the terms spelled out in the mortgages we signed. We may even be guilty of not knowing that there were laws in place to protect us against lending fraud, like the Truth in Lending Act and the Real Estate Settlement Procedures Act. But to say we were the greedy ones in this housing crisis is just wrong. If Allen and I (who have over a decade of experience in the title industry) didn't know that our loan was going to be securitized in an investment scam, how would the average homeowner know?

The middle class are the ones paying the price for the greed of Wall Street. Cleveland, Ohio, can lay claim to the picture of the year (2008 by Anthony Suau) in which a foreclosure deputy sheriff actually entered people's homes with a gun drawn. Americans have been thrown out of their homes, their credit has been destroyed, and their lives and that of their children have been changed forever. They are left with nothing while the brokers on Wall Street receive million-dollar bonuses in addition to their over-the-top wages! The average yearly salary for a Wall Street investment CEO is between ten and twenty million dollars. However, I did not see deputy sheriffs going into the big investment banks with guns drawn.

© Anthony Suau

CHAPTER 5

Securitization and Mortgage-Backed Securities

MORTGAGE-BACKED SECURITIES HAVE been around for a long time. If you talk to any investment broker, they will tell you that securities backed by real estate were always a stable and sound investment for your portfolio. What made them so secure was that people hardly ever defaulted on their traditional thirty-year fixed mortgages. When we were growing up, if you wanted to buy a home, you had to have at least 20 percent cash for the down payment, a steady income, and money in the bank. This meant you personally had a lot of money invested in the home you were buying. This may account for the fact that only about 1 percent of all mortgages written before 2008 ever defaulted.

After World War II, America's middle class began to grow at an unprecedented rate. In the 1950s and 1960s, there were plenty of manufacturing jobs and construction jobs in this country building homes for the rising middle class. The president at that time was Dwight D. Eisenhower, and he commissioned the building of our federal highway system. This not only created thousands of construction jobs building roads and bridges, but it also gave a tremendous boost to the automobile industry.

The American Dream was a typical family owning their own home and an automobile, like a station wagon. During summer vacation, Dad and Mom and the family would load up the station wagon and hit the highways to see America. It was a time unlike any other in our country's history. People had good-paying steady jobs and were able to make their monthly house payment without any worries.

What happened to the stable and sound investment of the mortgage-backed security? What happened between 1997 and 2008 when the crash occurred? I think the weakening of the Glass-Steagall Banking Act of 1933 may have played a part. Glass-Steagall was a reaction to the Great Depression and was supposed to protect us in the future from another collapse of Wall Street. The collapse of 1929 had an impact on economies all over the world, and not just in America. But in 1999, the Gramm-Leach-Bliley Act (also known as the Financial Services Modernization Act of 1999) altered all that.

Under this modernization act, commercial banks were allowed to merge with investment banks and insurance companies. This was a lot of financial power concentrated in a few institutions and contributed to the mentality of "too big to fail." So how did this new modernization act affect us, the average homeowner?

In the old days, you would go to your local community bank to get a home mortgage to purchase your first home. The bank was federally regulated by the Federal Reserve and had to have a certain amount of money in cash reserves to lend money. The bank would originate the loan and lend thousands of dollars to you, the borrower. In doing so, the bank retained all the risk of default if you couldn't pay back your mortgage. The loan paperwork (the note and the mortgage) was so important that the banker kept it in his vault in case he had to foreclose on you for nonpayment of the mortgage.

The Financial Services Modernization Act of 1999 profoundly changed how we conducted banking in this country. It allowed for the securitization of mortgage as investments with very little oversight. The amount of mortgage-backed securities by 2007 was $7.3 trillion. But how could they do this with a cash reserve required by the Federal Reserve? Wouldn't these investment banks on Wall Street who were writing all this business have to have millions or billions of dollars on reserve to lend out $7.3 trillion? No, they were not required to have any cash reserves on hand!

The Federal Reserve Bank chairman, Alan Greenspan, who served from 1987 to 2006, even admitted in an interview that even he didn't quite understand all the aspects of the new derivatives market created on Wall Street. The Federal Reserve was supposed to be the super regulator of Wall Street, and they just seemed to turn their heads and let the investment brokers do what they wanted to do. The impact of what was done by the Wall Street derivatives market is yet to be fully understood.

Just know that in the world, $590 trillion of derivatives have been written, and the entire global economy is estimated at only $60 trillion. Simply put, if the world's investors tried to cash in their derivatives valued at $590 trillion, there wouldn't be enough money in all the economies on earth to pay them. In my opinion (and I am not an economist), this would be a crash of catastrophic proportions.

But the investment banks on Wall Street got away with securitizing $7.3 trillion of mortgages in this country. Here is how it happened, as explained by Neal Garfield, Esq., and Brad Kaiser in one of their seminars. The investment bankers on Wall Street came up with a plan to sell forward. What this means is that they would sell mortgage-backed securities to get investor money before there were even any mortgages signed by you, the borrower. Neal so succinctly put it, "This is fraud, pure and simple. You are selling something that you do not have for money."

The investors might be your 401k mutual fund or your parents' pension fund or a hedge fund. These investors would be shopping around for investments for all the money they had collected from you every time you put money into your 401K plan. They wanted a certain return on their investment, say 5 percent. For every dollar they put into a mortgage-backed security investment, they wanted 5 cents in interest. According to Neal, Wall Street brokers said to themselves, "How can we provide a 5 percent return on investment without really paying out 5 percent?" They did some simple math and said, "This hedge fund wants $50,000 a year in interest return." So 5 percent of what number will equal $50,000? Using the high school algebra you learned (that you thought you would never have any use for) will help you find the number:

$0.05x = \$50,000$
$x = \$50,000 \text{ divided by } 0.05$
$x = \$1,000,000$

5 percent of $1 million will yield a $50,000 return on investment for the hedge fund. The hedge fund manager was willing to write a check for $1 million to the Wall Street investment bank to get a $50,000 interest return per year.

Now you come along and want a $300,000 mortgage for your home. The investment bank funds the $300,000 loan from the $1,000,000 received from the hedge fund.

That leaves the bank with $700,000. They put aside $50,000 in a reserve account to pay the hedge fund their 5 percent return on investment. The Wall Street investment bank is left with $650,000 in profit, and they haven't put up one red cent! And they don't pay any taxes on the profit either. This was the ultimate in Ponzi schemes! The hedge fund was getting paid back with its own money!

This is what happened to our mortgage when it was securitized. Our loan was doomed to fail from the beginning in order for the Ponzi scheme to continue. Wall Street had to make sure that our mortgage was a part of a short-term investment. Wall Street was paying investors back with their own money, and the reserves put aside with the investors' own money would eventually run out if the Ponzi scheme went on for years.

When ███████████████ told us they were going to crush us, it emboldened us, and we planned as if we were going to war. Allen and I would have long conversations about what happened in our situation and came to the conclusion that Wall Street wanted to turn our home, our most valuable asset, into a repo con. They wanted to treat our home like a car that gets repossessed and resold. The con would be to take our home to sheriff's sale once the loan failed and resell it and start the cycle all over again with a new homeowner. This repo scheme was contingent upon us just giving up and walking away from the financial mess they created. Well, we did not give up, and we did not walk away from our home. We continued to gain knowledge of securitization, and we stood firm in our resolve.

Securitization flow charts became a part of our battle plan. They can be detailed and confusing, and we would have to understand them to win (see Appendix A). In the four years since the housing market collapsed, more and more information has been put forth, and even the most complex securitization flow charts might need more updating. What happened to our mortgage when it was securitized can be summed up as follows:

> *Mortgagors* (the borrowers, Allen and I decide to obtain a mortgage refinance in 2005)
> *Originator* (we decide to obtain funds from Ameriquest Mortgage Company, who processes the paperwork and "funds" the loan)
> *Seller* (the entity that purchases the loans from the originator Ameriquest Mortgage Company and forms a pool of loans, usually five thousand goes into a pool)

Depositor (creates the issuing entity)

Trust fund (holds the pool of loans and issues certificates)

Trustee ███████████ Trust represents the investors and their interests in the pool of loans called mortgage-backed securities; also calculates the cash flow and pays out revenues)

Investors (hedge funds, mutual funds, pension funds, companies who buy the mortgage-backed securities as defined in the certificates; in our case, the investor in the Ameriquest Mortgage Securities Inc., Asset-Backed Pass-Through Certificates, Series 2005-R6 was a company named Cedefast)

Underwriters (they have sold the certificates to the investors, and they collect the money from the investors and send the money collected back up through the chain to the depositor, who sends the money to the seller, who sends the money to the originator, who sends the money to you, the borrower)

You then make your monthly house payment to a master servicer who sends your payment down the chain to the trustee who sends the money to the investors.

What was unique to this period in our financial history is that the securitization Ponzi scheme had Wall Street brokers selling forward, which meant they were selling something they did not yet possess. They had piles of cash but no signed mortgages. As it was once described to me, "It was a pile of money chasing mortgage paper." As we studied more, it became clear that it wasn't a case where all, out of the blue, millions of middle-class families suddenly had a need to borrow money to purchase their dream homes and sought funds with these mortgage companies. It was quite the opposite. The investment banks on Wall Street needed mortgage paper; they needed the signatures of millions of borrowers to carry out the con.

I remember receiving advertisements in the mail every day during the housing boom, informing me that we were prequalified for loans. To the point of overkill, television, radio, and even Internet advertising kept blaring that we could cash out the equity in our homes to pay off debt or to improve our homes by adding that new kitchen we had always wanted! They even went as far as selling us the perception that we could even send our children off to expensive Ivy League colleges with the funds obtained with their refinancing deals. It all made perfect sense to me now. The Wall Street swarm desperately needed me and millions of others like Allen and

I to sign mortgages to successfully keep this securitization "Ponzimonium" (a new word created as a result of all the pandemonium created around Ponzi schemes at this time in our history) swindle going.

It is very important to remember that the only person or persons who put up any cash for your loan to buy your first home or to refinance it was the investor. Everyone else in the securitization chain is just performing a task of either moving paperwork along or moving money up or down the chain. None of the people between you and the investor put up one red cent for your mortgage and have no legal right to file a foreclosure action on you if you should default. If Allen and I had chosen to walk away from our home, we would have walked away from over $220,410. This amount represents (as seen in Appendix B) our down payment, our closing costs, taxes, insurance, and all our house payments made.

There were articles at the time that cast aspersions on homeowners who opposed their foreclosures. If a homeowner won a foreclosure against a pretender lender, the court would issue the borrower a marketable title or a deed with the cloud on title removed. The authors of these articles would say the borrowers fought only to get a free house. But who really got a free house? The pretender lenders would have gotten a free house because they didn't put up one penny for your original loan!

CHAPTER 6

Securitization: Right and Wrong

WHEN WE DECIDED to refinance our home in 2005, our lender was Ameriquest Mortgage Company. What we didn't know at the time is that they did not put up any of the money for our loan. Not only that, when we did start making our payments in April 2005 on our refinance, Ameriquest Mortgage Company didn't receive our money. As a matter of fact, once we signed our paperwork in March, Ameriquest Mortgage Company immediately sold our loan to a mortgage broker. The lender Ameriquest made an immediate profit on our loan. They no longer had any skin in the game when it came to our mortgage!

The height of securitization was from 2001 to 2008, and it wasn't being done truthfully by the Wall Street investment banks. They had created a plan that financially benefited them at our expense. I remember Allen and I signing our loan papers and initialing over thirty pages that day. Our meeting was in a beautiful office building on Rockside Road in Cleveland, Ohio. When you came into the building, you were immediately greeted by a stunning sculpture of two blue herons done in silver. Their wings were outstretched magnificently as if to say, "Welcome, Terry and Allen! Your future awaits, and all your dreams will come true." We didn't know this day would become a nightmare within a few short years. This day may be better remembered as a fraudulent trap in which this lender had us sign our names to what we thought was an old-fashioned mortgage, but it really was a Wall Street scam to securitize our mortgage and put our home at a terrible risk.

Being title examiners for over a decade, we were surprised when the young man handling our loan said it wasn't necessary to have our signatures witnessed. We had always been trained that a mortgage should be signed, witnessed, and notarized. SWAN was the acronym we used to remember these actions. These steps had been performed for years in the title business. Property was always conveyed in an ethical manner for hundreds of years, but not now. These few additional steps would take too much time. Looking back now, this young man doing our closing just told us what we wanted to hear about this signing, and he completely disregarded the Truth in Lending Act. The swarms of brokers on Wall Street needed mortgages as quickly as possible to meet the worldwide demand for mortgage-backed securities and collateralized debt obligations.

We purchased a report by a company called Lumina Q to see if we could find out who really lent us the money for our loan. Ameriquest Mortgage Company went out of business in 2007 and had sold our mortgage loan to someone, and we wanted to know to whom. Lumina Q is a securitization research company copyrighted by Neil F. Garfield and portions copyrighted by DTC Systems Inc. and Daniel M. Edstrom. We could hardly stand the wait to get our report. Maybe the mystery of to whom we might owe some money (if any money was still owed) would be revealed in this report.

The day finally arrived when our report was delivered, and like kids on Christmas morning, we opened our package with great care. It was eight hundred pages long! Allen and I looked at each other and gasped. How did our little thirty page mortgage turn into an eight-hundred-page behemoth? We started reading, and on page four of our report, we saw names that were now becoming somewhat familiar to us from all our study. Here was our securitization chain. We saw who the originator, seller and master servicers were. We saw the name of the depositor, the issuing entity, and the trustee. We even saw names affiliated with our loan that we recognized from the nightly news, like Bear, Stearns & Co., Inc., Goldman Sachs & Company, Credit Suisse First Boston, LLC and the most notorious name of all, ▇▇▇▇▇▇▇ Securities Inc.

But we did not see the name of our creditor or investor who had put up the money for our loan. We read through all eight hundred pages of our report from Neil and Daniel only to be a little disappointed. Not disappointed in their work, but because we realized how secretive Wall Street had been in burying the information we needed to know to save our home. Neil Garfield's opinion was that Wall Street may not have even known who our creditor was or didn't really care to know who they were or maybe that they were hiding something! He said it was most likely all three.

Securitization, done right, would have disclosed the investor/creditor to the borrowers at the closing of the loan. In the days when securitized mortgages were done with openness and transparency, Allen and I, as borrowers, would have known that our mortgage was going to be securitized. We would have known that the mortgage we signed with one company was going to be sold to another company the very next day as an investment on Wall Street. We would have been given the names, addresses, phone numbers, and e-mails of the investor's contacts at the closing of the loan.

Then during the period of our loan, we would have received the same paperwork on the loan as the investor. All our loan activity would have been reported in an accounting spreadsheet. Allen and I would be equal partners with the investors. Securitization done right would disclose it all: current balances, payments, and any third-party payouts from credit default swaps. Can you image that? They would have openly disclosed any third-party payouts, if there had been any on our loan.

How would a default be handled under an open and transparent mortgage securitization? Allen and I would have notified the investor that we were in trouble and could not make our payments. The investors or the agents of the investors would meet as a group and take up the matter and decide as a group to either work out a solution with Allen and me or to foreclose our loan. But the difference between securitization done right and what we experienced in our securitization done wrong was light years apart.

We knew that down the road, we were going to meet ████████ in a court of law and we needed to suit up. Our defense was to continue to make sense out of the complexities of securitization. We continually asked ourselves what these pretender lenders did that was so wrong. What we found next absolutely astonished us. In no uncertain terms, they broke the law, plain and simple.

In an article posted on LivingLies.com, written by Christopher Story, he explained that the securitization of our home mortgage was illegal under United States law and common law. He went on to say this:

> Securitization is illegal under US legislation—primarily because it is fraudulent and causes specific violations of RICO, usury, Antitrust and bankruptcy laws. And it flies in the face of public policy in numerous ways, as is expounded in extensive detail in an analysis to be published in the journal *Economic Intelligence Review* 2009 Q1 (7) with several pages of book, article, and case references.

The mortgage we signed in 2005 was illegal and violated RICO laws! Wasn't RICO always mentioned with federal racketeering? How did this apply to us here in Cleveland, Ohio? We had to learn more. First thing was to learn what this acronym stands for. It is the Racketeer Influenced and Corrupt Organizations Act, and it is federal legislation developed to break up organized crime in the United States. Did this mean the Gambino crime family was involved in my mortgage? The answer was a resounding no, but when Wall Street securitized my mortgage, they were guilty of violating many of the codes of the RICO Act. According to the article on LivingLies.com, Christopher Story went on to name the specific sections violated:

> The specific RICO sections are: Section 1341 (mail fraud); Section 1343 (wire fraud); Section 1344 (financial institution fraud); Section 1957 (engaging in monetary transactions improperly derived from specific unlawful activity) ('the money you make from the illegal exploitation of my money, is my money'); and Section 1952 (racketeering).

I was astounded when I read this, especially the part that says "the money you make from the illegal exploitation of my money is my money!" All the money Wall Street made on my home loan, perhaps as much as $18 million, under Section 1957 of the Racketeer Influenced and Corrupt Organizations Act, was mine? There aren't enough hours and days left in my life to spend $18 million, but if Allen and I could get a judge in Cuyahoga County to make a ruling in our favor for a sum that unbelievably large, it would create a precedent in the law that could open the proverbial "floodgates." Can you just imagine how much money they would have to pay out if all the middle-class families facing foreclosure took a stand and fought for their homes? It was a goal well worth pursuing in a court of law. It made us even stronger and more determined to stand and fight our impending foreclosure.

CHAPTER 7

A Tangled Web:
A Few Words about MERS

JUST HOW FAR would the Wall Street mega banks and all their minions take this scam against all of us?

One morning, as was our custom, Allen came out of his home office with a delight in his step and a stack of research in his hands. "Ter, you aren't going to believe this one!" he said. "What I found out this morning will boggle your mind. You know how we kept seeing Mortgage Electronic Registration Systems Inc. as nominee for such and such bank on many of the mortgages we pulled for our title exams? This company was formed to deal with all the original mortgages and notes Wall Street didn't want to deal with and just destroyed. So when the mega bank needed assignments, they just had them created and signed by robo-signers." (see Appendix C)

Amazingly, MERS accomplished everything described in the previous paragraph with about forty-five employees. But over twenty thousand other people paid MERS Inc. $25 for the right to call themselves vice president and use the *MERS* name on their mortgages and assignments. This is how, for example, any of us could be delivering pizzas one day and then sign hundreds of mortgage assignments as a vice president of a bank the next day with little or no training. These MERS vice presidents became a class of employees known as robo-signers. MERS is an acronym for Mortgage Electronic Registration Systems and was created in 1993 by the Mortgage Bankers Association. Ginnie Mae, Fannie Mae, Freddie Mac, and several other financial entities in the real estate industry saw the value of using MERS Inc. as a time-saving approach to dealing with the filing of documents.

It was set up to track beneficial interests in and the servicing rights to mortgage loans on behalf of *member* banks. MERS is well suited to the present-day securitization of mortgages. It can move *copies* of documents electronically at high rates of speed, which in turn saves vast amounts of time. As years went by, the Wall Street banking system believed that the MERS method of recordation eliminated the need to warehouse original documents. By destroying these original documents, the Wall Street banks saved millions of dollars in storage fees and millions of man hours to retrieve these documents. It was not long before MERS stopped recording their assignments of mortgages in the local records offices throughout the United States. This saved them even more millions and millions of dollars in recording fees. When foreclosures began to pile up in mid-2005, MERS became the designated servicer that filed foreclosure lawsuits against borrowers.

All this was done without changing a single law in any of the fifty states. As more and more foreclosures began to pile up, MERS bluffed their way through foreclosure courts by presenting copies of original documents. This worked to perfection until a few borrowers stood up to these foreclosure fanatics who wanted to have control over the activities of everyone and challenged the documents presented in foreclosure court. To counter these brazen borrowers—how dare they challenge the bank!—MERS began to hire robo-signers and bought high-tech signature machines. This is a dangerous game that MERS is playing in many state courts throughout the United States. If they ever dare to take one of these types of foreclosure cases to trial by jury and *lose*, the results will be beyond cataclysmic for the Wall Street bankers!

We looked further into the Securities and Exchange Commission website and clearly saw that MERS was not a part of any SEC filing. It would have trouble establishing legal standing when challenged by borrowers in court, as it cannot establish a clean chain of title. MERS would make it nearly impossible for new buyers of a foreclosed home to get title insurance and would prevent property owners from resolving property disputes without having to file lawsuits. David E. Woolley of the Harbinger Analytics Group in Tustin, California, said that the MERS system may have a complete destructive effect on over four hundred years of recorded property rights in the United States. More bad news was delivered by Professor Alan M. White of the Valparaiso University School of Law when he matched ownership records from MERS to public domain records and found out that fewer than 30 percent of mortgages had an accurate record in MERS. What is really troublesome is that MERS holds over 60 million mortgages in the United States. This is over half of all US mortgages.

What has really hurt MERS mortgages is that a number of states have rulings at the Appeals Court and Supreme Court level that have stripped MERS of foreclosure rights because of its defective paperwork. This has occurred in states such as Vermont, Florida, Ohio, Massachusetts, New York, and Kansas. The Kansas Supreme Court ruling in *Landmark National Bank v. Kesler* states that MERS has no right or standing to bring an action of foreclosure. In fact, the MERS mess is so widespread in all fifty states that homeowners that are not in foreclosure and have nothing to do with a MERS mortgage are affected. If your next-door neighbor has a MERS mortgage, it could affect your ability to sell your home—whether the neighbor is in foreclosure or not! If there is a property dispute between you and this neighbor, then you will have to sue him in a court of law to have a judge decide where the correct property line exists. If this is not done before you try to sell your house, then the buyer of your home may not be able to purchase title insurance. Should the buyer not be able to get title insurance, your deal could be rescinded by your title company. Issues like these could affect about thirty million more mortgages in the United States. This would make a total of more than ninety million residential mortgages that could be negatively affected by MERS. This is about 75 percent of all residential mortgages in the United States. Unbelievable!

After my husband and I learned about the vast negative consequences of dealing with MERS, we decided that we should be absolutely sure that our mortgage was not involved with MERS. Since we both have over ten years of experience at various levels within the title industry, we knew that MERS would be mentioned on the first page of our mortgage. We looked at our mortgage and looked for the words *Mortgage Electronic Registration Systems Inc.* as nominee for Ameriquest Mortgage Company. We were relieved that ours was not a MERS loan. However, it is possible for the mortgage to have been registered with MERS after the mortgage was filed with the recorder's office. We visited the MERS website to find out if they had any information about our mortgage loan. We typed in www.MERSInc.org to access their website. The home page came up, and we clicked on MERS FOR HOMEOWNERS in the left-hand column. When the next page came up, we scrolled to the bottom of the page. We clicked on the blue phrase MERS FCRA secure portal. The next page said

"Welcome to MERSCORP Inc." We clicked on "for first time users click here." On the next page, we created a new account. After the creation of our account, we could ask questions about our loan. We asked them if there was any record of our loan with MERS. They communicated back that there was not any record of us or any mortgage loan! It was a good day for us. But what about our neighbors' mortgages? Were any of them involved with MERS Inc.? That would be a worry for another day. Oh, what a tangled web of deceit MERS has woven for all of us.

CHAPTER 8

The SEC:
A Modern Akashic Record

THE SECURITIES AND Exchange Commission (SEC) was created in 1934. Its purpose was the enforcement of the Securities Act of 1933. In 2005, our loan was placed into a securitized trust and filed with the SEC. However, my husband and I were not aware that our loan was securitized until after the pretender lender foreclosed on our property in late 2008. At that time, we learned that our loan was securitized and that it had been placed into a pool of loans. With this newly discovered information, we were able to find out a great deal about what happened to our loan after we closed it on March 23, 2005. Eventually, we found that the Ameriquest Mortgage Securities Trust 2005-R6 had been filed with the SEC. We searched the SEC on its website at www.SEC.gov. There was a gold mine of information available to us. At first, we paged through this website for hours before all this information began making some sense to us. Later, we realized that the SEC conducted very little, if any, oversight concerning our securities loan transaction. From our prospective, it was obvious that this vast amount of information had been kept secret from us for years. This knowledge was hidden from us behind the illusionary veil called the residential home mortgage. When we began to unravel the details of our securitized loan, we knew that we had discovered information that would help us win our foreclosure case.

It was as if we had awakened from a prolonged and deep sleep. We felt enlightened and confident in our battle with ██████████████████ ██████. The term *the sleeping profit* came to mind. We slept while ████████ ██████ *profited*. Somehow, this realization seemed familiar to us!

While the SEC was being formed in 1934, another influential entity became part of the public consciousness during the 1930s. It was the work of Edgar Cayce or the true "sleeping prophet." He could access all knowledge from a *universal supercomputer* while in a trance-like state. This mystical compendium existed in an ether state, and Cayce referred to it as the akashic records. These records contained all human knowledge and the history of the cosmos. The records are constantly updated automatically. People other than Edgar Cayce have been trained to access these records through astral projection or by being placed into deep hypnosis. It appears that the akashic records have another similarity to the SEC records; they seem to be completely unregulated. As my husband and I do not know anything about astral projection and have never been placed into a deep hypnotic trance, we had no way of knowing about our loan being filed with the SEC before foreclosure. This lack of knowledge put us at a great disadvantage during the preforeclosure process called loan modification.

We found navigating the SEC website to be routine once we figured out what documents were important to us in our foreclosure defense. All filings with the SEC involving our loan were made by the trustee ██████████████████████. Accessing the documents available to us is much easier today than when we started searching the SEC about five years ago. This is made possible by the activation of the online database known as EDGAR. This is the Electronic Data Gathering, Analysis, and Retrieval system. I don't believe that the name of this retrieval system has anything to do with Edgar Cayce. Just a coincidence, I guess.

Important documents that we studied for our foreclosure defense included the prospectus, the pooling and servicing agreement (PSA), Form 10-Q, Form 10-K, Form 8-K and Form 15. The prospectus provided details and facts about our securities offering that an investor would need to make an informed investment decision. The pooling and servicing agreement (PSA) explains the responsibilities and rights of the servicer, the trustee, and other financial entities that oversee a pool of mortgage loans that includes our own mortgage. Form 10-Q is a quarterly financial report. Form 10-K is the annual financial report. Form 8-K is an interim report which announces any material event or corporate change that occurred between quarterly reports (10-Q). Finally, Form 15 is filed when the trustee claims that the number of investors has fallen to twelve or less and that the trustee no longer has to file *any reports*.

Form 15 is also filed by the trustee when the trust in question had been dissolved. If the trust has been dissolved, then how is it possible for the trustee to foreclose on anyone? The total SEC filing contained over eight hundred pages. I printed it out myself, but it used up a great deal of ink. It took several hours to print as I had to keep resupplying the paper tray. But this is well worth the time and effort if you are facing a foreclosure on your home and you do not have the money to purchase a report from a company like Lumina Q.

The prospectus provided us with important facts about the role of the depositor in our securitization chain. All mortgages must pass through the depositor by true sale before being sold to the trust, again, by true sale. A true sale would mean that our mortgage was sold from the originator to the seller to the depositor and then to the trust. This would be proven by having the original note being received, accepted, and signed as it passed through each of the four financial entities. This would be evidenced by the original note having three endorsements on the face of the last page. Then the mortgage would have the chain of assignments that matched the endorsements. We went to the county recorder's office to look for our assignments from the originator to the seller, and there were none! There was no assignment recorded from the seller to the depositor either. This was very odd, and something was wrong. The prospectus clearly stated what events needed to be recorded in the public records, and we found absolutely nothing.

The pooling and servicing agreement (PSA) was another area in the SEC filing that proved to be a treasure trove of information that could be used in our foreclosure defense. There were a few sections that helped us understand when the pretender lender ███████████████████████ was either lying to us or trying to run an elaborate con. In section 2.01, we learned that the trustee ████████████████████████████████ has no interest in any of the assets in the trust itself. Section 2.02 showed us that the trustee cannot act outside the scope of the pooling and servicing agreement. The information from these two sections alone would allow us to raise issues with the court about the rights of the trustee to claim any title or interest in the trust. Section 2.05 taught us that the trustee is required to receive a valid chain of assignments concerning mortgages. In section 2.08, it states that all original notes must be acquired by true sale. These two sections would allow us to raise issues with the court concerning a defective chain of title. Section 3.04 explains that the servicer—Citi-Residential—was reimbursed for advances to the trust.

Section 4.03 talks about the servicer being indemnified against any monetary losses to the trust. These last two sections were very important to us as we could raise serious issues concerning damages or monetary loss if our foreclosure ever went to trial.

It is important to know how to navigate the SEC website as many people facing foreclosure may not be as fortunate as my husband and I. As time went on, we began to acquire more resources to fight back. It has been our experience that if you fight the good fight, good things will start to fall your way. We were able to spend money and time to print out our first copy of the SEC filings. Later on, we invested some money in acquiring a forensics report from Neil Garfield. This good fortune began when the pretender lenders absolutely refused to accept partial payments on our mortgage. In any event, it is important to find out how to access the SEC website as anyone can find out about the securitization of their own loan.

To begin, you will have to type in www.SEC.gov, and under FILINGS, click on Search for Company Filings. On the next page that comes up, click on Company name or fund name. The next page will give you a box to type in the name of the trust. Go ahead and type in the full name or at least the first couple of words in the trust name. Then click on Find Companies. A screen will come up with the names of the several trusts as many ($7.3 trillion worth) were created over many years. In our case, it was Ameriquest Mortgage Securities Inc., Asset-Backed Pass-Through Certificates, Series 2005-R6 with a listing of about two dozen or so trusts. We easily found ours and clicked on the assigned trust number to the left of the trust name. Once you get into your specific trust, you will find that there is a lot of long but interesting work ahead of you. If you are dedicated to fighting your foreclosure, then you will find this information to be very rewarding.

An important concept that should be addressed at this point is that there exists at least three possible explanations about how your loan and ours were securitized. First, there is the explanation filed with the SEC. Second, there is another explanation filed in the Cuyahoga county foreclosure court. And third, there is what really happened in the securitization of your loan and mine. The last explanation will only become available through the discovery process should our case or yours ever goes to trial.

Remember that in order to locate the name of your trust, you must go to the county recorder's office either in person or online. There you will find an assignment to your mortgage that was filed just prior to or just after the date that you received the service of your foreclosure papers. This assignment will contain the name of your trust. It will more than likely be the first time that you are aware of the identity of this trust. If you are not in foreclosure and are just curious about knowing the name of the trust involved with your mortgage, then call the servicer that sends you a billing statement each month. Ask them to provide you with this information. If they refuse, then hire a competent securitization attorney as there may be trouble ahead.

CHAPTER 9

We Get Sued

ALLEN HAD FINALLY gone back to work in the late summer of 2008 delivering nuclear medicine. The doctor released him for work without restrictions. He was glad to be back working as he enjoyed the part he was playing in helping sick people get better. He said he had a much better perspective of what sick people went through with the time, the pain, and the energy spent to get well again. He thought his own financial situation at home would improve with another regular paycheck coming in.

Then the worst thing imaginable happened. While carrying the sixty-pound lead-lined case into a hospital in Lorain, Ohio, he felt something rip in his hand. He lost the grip he had around the case, and it dropped to the floor with a very loud bang. He felt immense pain in his hand and fingers and knew he must have ripped the tendons he had spent over a year healing. The doctor said he would need surgery on the hand, if he was ever going to be able to use it again. Surgery and another year of rehabilitation would destroy us financially, as our life's savings was now gone as we tried to make our house payments after his accident with the sixty-five-thousand-pound tractor trailer.

We knew that the lender wasn't interested in our reasons as to why we couldn't make our payments, but perhaps now, they would approve our loan modification application. We had tried to be proactive and contacted them soon after the truck hit Allen back in 2007. This was a year later and, still, no loan modification. Every time we filled out their paperwork, they would say that they had lost it and would we send it again. Or they would say they could not lower our payments or our interest rate or even determine which program we would qualify for until they got our papers, to which we replied, "We had sent them three times."

The most ridiculous reason we heard from Citi-Residential during this time was that they could not modify our loan until we were two months behind in our payments. We said we worked as title examiners in the foreclosure and loan modification business and never heard of such a thing. How could that be? We were trying to be responsible by developing a plan to avoid foreclosure.

Our ancestors must have been smiling down on us at that moment when Allen called the lender about reinjuring his hand—they agreed to approve our loan application. We filled out all the necessary additional information they requested of us and faxed it to the number they provided. We were jubilant at the prospect that maybe now we could work out a solution to this problem that benefited both the lender and us. We were so confident that the loan mod would work out, that we rerecorded our property deed so that it included survivorship language. It was better to be prepared in case there ever was another accident that affected one of us. At least the survivor would have a house to live in.

Days went by and then weeks, and we heard nothing from the lender. Late summer had turned to the time when yellow school buses noisily chugged up and down my street. It had now been three months since our last house payment, so our loan modification must be in the works by now. We were filled with hope that our long-awaited solution was on its way and it would help us end this financial nightmare. It was the night of the presidential election, and Barrack Obama was announced as our new president. He had campaigned on hope and change, and maybe, we hoped, our change was right around the corner too.

The next day, there was a knock on our door. I jumped up and ran to the door. It was most likely the UPS man or the FedEx man hand delivering our loan mod papers! I was pumped and still feeling all the hope from the night before. I opened the door, and there at my doorstep was a lady from the sheriff's department with a badge on her jacket. She had a package of papers in one hand while her other hand was at her side touching a gun in a holster. When I saw the badge and the gun, I knew this wasn't good, and all the hope I had been feeling vanished.

Allen had also heard the knock and came flying down the stairs. We had just been discussing earlier that morning how excited we were that any day our loan mod papers would be here. He stood in quiet disbelief and listened, as did I, to the deputy sheriff say that she was here on official business on behalf of ███████████. She handed me the package of papers; I signed my name in receipt, and she left. I tore them open. We had been sued for foreclosure!

We looked at each other in shock. Our hope moved to despair on the spot. We had made a big mistake trusting the lender for the past year, thinking they were going to modify our loan so we could stay in our home. They didn't care about us as people or Allen's truck accident. All they cared about was winning at any cost. This was the first step in the fight to crush us in a court of law.

We felt as if we had been duped by ██████████ and their servicer, Citi-Residential. They obviously had been stringing us along for over a year saying they would modify our mortgage, but in reality, they were just trying to run us out of money. They knew our savings were exhausted as we had openly told them. ██████████ also knew Allen wasn't working, and they most likely said to themselves, "How far could one middle-class family stretch one paycheck? There won't be any money left for the Rays to hire any legal help, and we will get this house!"

The foreclosure papers said we had twenty-eight days to respond to the complaint, or else our home would be sold at a sheriff's auction. We had to change our mindset immediately to defend our home, and we only had twenty-eight days. The enormity of such a task was unbelievable, but Allen and I would not quit now. The measure of a person is how they act not when times are good, but when times are bad.

We were extremely low on cash, and we knew we needed a lawyer to file legal papers in response. Since there would be no cash settlement on this type of case, a lawyer taking our case on a contingency was off the table. Then I remembered that two of my coworkers had mentioned they were facing foreclosure on their own homes. I delicately struck up a conversation at work and asked them how they found the means to pay a lawyer to represent them. They told me they were using the legal plan at work. With all the stress of my personal financial situation and the clock now ticking on my house going to auction, I had forgotten that every two weeks I was having money taken out of my paycheck for legal coverage! I had legal coverage for the defense of my mortgage foreclosure! My drive home from work that evening seemed like an eternity. I couldn't wait to tell Allen the great news.

My husband was flabbergasted at my news, but he reminded me that every minute of every day counted. Even though the court said for us to respond within twenty-eight days, it was November 2008, which meant the courthouse would be closed for Thanksgiving. That was four days

TERRY PUFFER RAY & ALLEN RAY

completely gone because of the holiday. We had to subtract the weekends too. After all, the entire courthouse was closed on Saturday and Sunday. Our real deadline was more like sixteen days to find a lawyer who had knowledge of mortgage foreclosure defense, schedule an appointment when he or she had an opening, and get all the paperwork written and hand delivered to the court for the looming foreclosure. The response could not be late under any circumstance, or else we would lose our house in a sheriff's auction.

If we couldn't find the right lawyer and get our response to the court in time, all the physical pain Allen endured because of being struck by a semitruck, a year's worth of hospital stays as an inpatient, and then all the rehabilitation hoping to be normal again would have been in vain. I had endured the emotional impact of almost losing my husband and being widowed after thirty-two years of a good, strong marriage. I almost lost the best years to come in any marriage. All the pressure of working forty to fifty hours a week to keep my family together and to keep a roof over our heads was culminating in this moment—these sixteen days on the calendar.

We found a lawyer at the law firm of Oberholtzer & Filous, LPA in a quaint town in Medina, Ohio. The town is a step back into time with charming, restored original buildings from the middle of the last century. Both Allen and I had done many title searches in the county recorder's office there, as well as legal searches in the courthouse. It felt comfortable there and a little like home, so maybe a law firm from this town would work out. Mr. John C. Oberholtzer came to our home for the first meeting to review our mortgage and settlement papers. He sat in our living room and carefully looked over the papers. He immediately found discrepancies and even asked us to provide our title insurance policy. From my work at the title insurance company, I knew there was a big, big problem with our title if a lawyer was asking to see a title policy. John suggested we meet in his office in a few days.

We got an appointment that fit everyone's schedule, which was the good news. The bad news was that now we only had nine days to get our response to the court in Cuyahoga County. I could see Allen was really apprehensive that this would not get done in time. We met with Matthew G. Bruce, esquire of the firm. He was a good-looking young attorney. Allen explained what he had learned about the securitization of our home loan. I could tell that Matthew had a very sharp legal mind by some of the questions he asked us. But the way he was looking at Allen caused me some concern. It was if Allen was speaking a foreign language.

I honestly don't think Allen was aware of how his words and explanations were being received, which was good because he just kept talking. It made sense to me, as I had been studying for a year and a half right along with him. Now I was really nervous as it might come down to me interpreting what Allen had said so that Matthew could get on the same page as us concerning securitization of mortgages.

Then something so simple and wonderful happened. Allen recounted to the lawyer a telephone call in which the lender said, "Mr. Ray, we don't have the original note or mortgage. We destroyed it. We don't need it either to force you and your wife into foreclosure. Either pay up, or else . . ." The lawyer sat straight up, looked both Allen and me directly in the eye, and said forcefully, "They can't take your home into foreclosure if they don't have the original note and mortgage! I know exactly what to do to help you. I may not know as much as you about mortgage securitization yet, but I do know the law in this state. And no lender or bank can take your house away from you without presenting originals to the court to show that they are the true owner and holder of the note!"

We were stunned when we left that first meeting. We drove home that afternoon feeling a little relief. But the clock was still ticking, and we recognized that we only had eight days left. It took our law firm a week to write our response to the foreclosure. Allen had been calling every other day to make sure they were going to make the deadline. It was down to one day. The court had to have our response in Cleveland in one day. We were so nervous that it might get lost in the mail or not delivered by FedEx in time. Both of these businesses do a great job, but this was our home at stake. We wanted to be absolutely certain the papers were delivered and time stamped by the court. We offered to hand deliver the package ourselves and get the response time stamped. We had done this many times for other customers in our work as title examiners, so we were confident in our knowledge and abilities to get this task done right and in time.

"Well, what do you think? May we hand-deliver the papers to the court ourselves?" we asked the lawyer.

He assured us that he would get them there in time. That night, neither of us slept.

The next morning, we hungrily got online and went into the court's website to see if our response had been filed in time—on the very last day it could have been filed. There it was! ▮▮▮▮▮▮▮ v. Allen G. Ray et al., defendant's response!

The battle had begun.

CHAPTER 10

I Rather Enjoy
Taking People's Homes

THIS BATTLE TO save our home was beginning in the cruelest of months: January. As anyone who has ever lived in northeastern Ohio can tell you, winters can be brutal. In downtown Cleveland, the winds blow over frozen Lake Erie carrying bone-chilling cold. It seemed appropriate that our first meeting with ███████████ and their legal counsel was in January 2009.

We hurried to get from our car to the courthouse to avoid the bitter cold. What we didn't anticipate was how cold our opponent would be in this hearing. We saw a familiar face and calmed down a bit. It was Matthew Bruce, our attorney. All of us sat outside the magistrate's chamber exchanging pleasantries to break the tension. As you might expect for that time of year, Matthew asked us how our holidays had been. Tears welled up in my eyes as I tried to answer his question. "We weren't able to have a holiday this year, Matthew. We were so preoccupied on this hearing, and money has been very tight as you can imagine with Allen still not working." I could see in his face the impact my words had on him, so I stopped talking about our holidays. What I did see was a young attorney with empathy and compassion. In that moment, I knew we had hired the right person for this battle.

The wait made me so nervous as I anticipated what the opposing counsel might look like or what they might say about us. Then a woman came out to the waiting room and said the magistrate would see us now. All my questions were about to be answered. Allen, Matthew, and I proceeded into Chief Magistrate Stephen M. Bucha III's chambers.

There was a substantial wooden table in the middle of the room. At the head of the table sat Magistrate Bucha in a power position watching us come in. I looked to one side of the table, and there sat the opposing counsel—James L. Sassano of Carlisle, McNellie, Rini, Kramer, & Ulrich Co., LPA. My first question was now answered. He was an older man with thinning gray hair. Allen and our attorney sat across from Attorney Sassano, as Allen wanted to look this man directly in the face. My husband is built for these situations and is fearless. It is one of the things I admire about him most—his courage. I sat at the opposite end of the table down from the magistrate. I am the observer and listener in our family, and this gave me the best vantage point to take in this meeting.

The magistrate had the complaint of foreclosure in front of him as well as our response. He had James Sassano begin. My second question was about to be answered. He presented the facts of his case, saying we were in default and hadn't met his client's demands for payment in full. Mr. Sassano had even brought a final judicial report to this hearing. A final judicial report is a complete title exam on a home showing any liens, either voluntary or involuntary, against the property. It shows the deed chain of all the previous owners as well as the deed of the current owner. The legal description of the property is very important in a judicial report. The court must make sure they are foreclosing on the correct property. He ended by demanding that the court order our home to be sold at the next sheriff's auction. It is one thing to read about people's homes being sold at auction, but to hear the actual words about your own home is startling.

It was now our turn. Matthew Bruce presented our side and informed the magistrate about all our efforts to try and obtain a loan modification as far back as July 2007. He showed all our communications via faxes and e-mails to the bank. He showed our accounting sheet we had put together showing our assets and liabilities. Matthew even told the magistrate that all our creditors had worked with us to lower our interest rates and our monthly payments. Some of the banks to whom we owed money actually took partial payments. All the banks worked with us except ██████ ██████!

Allen now had the opportunity to speak about the state of affairs that brought us to this hearing. He told Magistrate Bucha about the truck hitting him on the interstate on July 10, 2007. These were circumstances beyond our control, and we felt our only hope was to have the court supervise the bank and the loan modification on our home.

Something Allen said set James Sassano off, and he abruptly stood up and exclaimed, "But the Rays haven't paid my client in three years!"

The magistrate looked at Sassano, astonished to see such an unprofessional reaction by an attorney. Quickly, Magistrate Bucha looked down at his papers and went through them methodically, page by page. We sat quietly, wondering what would happen next. We thought Attorney Sassano's statement was brazen and arrogant. Not only was it untrue, but it was meant to impugn our characters. After all, it was ███████████ who had said they were going to crush us in a court of law. We shouldn't have been shocked by this arrogant pronouncement.

Before our attorney could object, the magistrate said, "According to the records I have here, the Rays are only five months behind in their payments, not three years. I am going to order the attorneys to work together and come to an agreement after this hearing on a loan modification for Mr. and Mrs. Ray. This will be under the court's supervision, and final loan modification papers are to be presented at a hearing set for May 2009. This hearing is dismissed."

The Cuyahoga County court system for foreclosure prevention worked very well for us. Magistrate Bucha's goal was to be fair to the parties, us and the lender. A loan mod would allow us to stay in our house and put this insanity behind us. Knowing the bank as we did now, it would allow them to avoid the embarrassment of not having the original note and mortgage.

A bank—or, in our case, a pretender lender—cannot take your home if they do not have the original note and mortgage. They would also have to have the legal standing and legal capacity to follow through with the foreclosure. Magistrate Bucha seemed to follow the Boyko model. This model was named after the judge Christopher A. Boyko, who is *the* federal judge in the United States District Court Northern District of Ohio that began ruling against the Wall Street mega banks in 2006 right here in Cleveland, Ohio. I am so proud of my city and its legal community for all their hard work in standing up for middle-class families facing foreclosure. In Judge Boyko's stunning decision on October 2007, he told the mega player ███████████ that their legal arguments of legal standing fell woefully short.

Interpretation: if you are not the owner and holder of the note, you own nothing. This is what is referred to as the Boyko model, and it might help us if this loan modification didn't work and we had to go to trial. The judge's ruling of stopping the Wall Street mega banks at the gate set a powerful precedent in the law that protected the homeowners who chose to stay in their homes and fight for their rights under the law. Our mediation conference was set for May, and we were studying and diligently preparing for that day. We had four months till then, and so much was happening with foreclosures between 2008 and 2009. You couldn't go one day without some news of a pro se litigant (without legal counsel) or a homeowner represented by counsel having success in fighting their foreclosures. Allen and I were hoping and praying for our own success, and we were prepared mentally to go to trial in a state court or even a federal court if the loan modification conference didn't go well.

We found an important case that definitely would help us. It was *Wells Fargo Bank, NA v. Oties Jordan, et al.* Oties and Sylvia Jordan lived in our area (see Appendix D) and were pro se litigants fighting a foreclosure on a piece of property located on Wade Park Avenue in Cleveland. They signed a mortgage and a note with Delta Funding Corporation on January 3, 2003. Wells Fargo Bank filed a complaint for money judgment, foreclosure, and relief on August 3, 2007. Here is where it gets very interesting. The Jordans had signed with Delta Funding Corporation, so why was Wells Fargo Bank filing the foreclosure? We knew enough now from our research and our professions that there must have been an assignment filed from Delta Funding as assignor to Wells Fargo Bank as assignee. We immediately went into title examiner mode and searched the Cuyahoga County records for an assignment. What we found was astonishing. The complaint for foreclosure was filed with the court before Wells Fargo Bank was the assignee of record! That meant that Wells Fargo did not have the legal standing to file this complaint. The complaint was filed on August 3, 2007, and the assignment of record was not recorded until August 22, 2007.

The lower court overlooked this very important matter concerning legal standing and ruled against the Jordans. But Oties and Slyvia Jordan were smart enough to realize that this was not right and filed an appeal with the Court of Appeals of Ohio, Eighth Appellate District. They filed as pro se litigants for a second time against Wells Fargo Bank. Wells Fargo hired the law firm of Shapiro, Van Ess, Phillips & Barragate, LLP. Phil Barragate, Esq. was one of my former employers. He and I worked together at Shapiro & Felty, LLP for about three years. I never was very impressed with his legal mind or his work at Shapiro. Now he was working on this critical appeal with Attorney Benjamin D. Carnahan as legal counsel for Wells Fargo Bank, NA.

On April 21, 2009, the Court of Appeals ruled against Wells Fargo Bank, NA, saying, "There is no evidence in the record that Wells Fargo Bank was the holder of the note on the date the complaint was filed. Motion by appellee for reconsideration is denied." Shapiro, Van Ess, Phillips & Barragate, LLP lost this critical decision for their client, Wells Fargo. They were beaten by a couple of pro se litigants named Oties and Sylvia Jordan.

I was more confident than ever about my upcoming hearing in May. Allen and I celebrated the Jordans' victory and vowed to follow their lead. All we had to do now was get our paperwork to Oberholtzer & Filous, LPA for Matthew Bruce to go over for his meetings with the opposing counsel for ████████████. That was easy enough as we had done this three times before and had a complete file folder full of our tax returns for two years, our banking statements for six months, our pay stubs, and our list of liabilities to our creditors. Now we waited for the day of reckoning.

At the end of April 2009, we received a call from Matthew Bruce. He informed us he would not be coming to the May premediation conference. He was instead sending a legal intern named Christopher L. Wetherbee who would walk us through the mediation. Christopher was still attending law school, and we heard he was a bright student. We hung up the phone and looked at each other, thinking this was odd. Why wouldn't Matthew be representing us that day? Had the behind-the-scenes talks with James Sassano gone that well? We discussed this twist and decided it didn't matter to us as we were prepared and ready for whatever would be thrown at us that day.

We arrived at the courthouse early that morning and got on the elevator to go to the fourth floor of the Justice Center to the Office for Alternative Dispute Resolution. We nervously signed in to let the mediator know we were present. We found a couple of seats next to each other and began our wait to be called. We didn't know what Christopher Wetherbee looked like, so we kept our eye on the door, studying each and every person who entered the waiting room.

The mediator's name for our hearing was Ann Mannen. The judge on our case was Timothy J. McGinty, and the magistrate was Stephen M. Bucha III. We were in the hands of three legal professional people with years of experience in the law. We were confident that a resolution would be worked out that was fair and equitable.

A young man came into the room and signed in and sat down a couple of seats from us. We didn't recognize him at all. All of a sudden, he got up when a woman entered. She looked like a judge (the way she was dressed), and he addressed her as Magistrate Mannen. Now we knew he was one of the key players, but for whom? They stood in conversation, and we listened intently, hoping to catch his name. We heard the name Brian Bly. Could this be the infamous Brian J. Bly—the robo-signer for Nationwide Title we had read about? What was a robo-signer doing at our mediation conference?

Magistrate Mannen said to him in a tone that was surprisingly emphatic, "I will be ready for your next case in a few minutes, Mr. Bly."

He acknowledged her, saying, "I will be ready."

She then said all, out of the blue, "I know this can't be easy for you, Mr. Bly, coming here every day to take people's homes from them."

Stunningly, he replied to her, "Knowing the kind of guy I am, I rather enjoy taking people's homes from them."

In an instant, her face went from empathy to shock. She turned away from him and walked down the hall, shaking her head. This was the moment of truth for Allen and me. We had come face-to-face with Mr. Brian L. Bly, the lawyer for ███████████, and not the infamous robo-signer. This Brian Bly embodied and represented the bank's attitude of complete and utter disdain for the borrower. Allen was seething. In my heart of hearts, I knew Brian L. Bly was about to be defenestrated if he wasn't careful.

My thoughts entering this battle with ███████████ and their chosen warrior, Brian L. Bly, were different than my husband's. I thought about family and our ancestors. Allen and I both come from a long line of impassioned individuals who fought against oppression. I am the tenth generation of George Puffer who came to America from England in the early 1600s. On February 24, 1640, he purchased twenty acres of land in Braintree, Massachusetts, upon which he built his home and began his family. The importance of property, family, and home has been passed down to me for over four hundred years.

My fifth great-grandfather, Jabez Puffer, fought in the American Revolution of 1776. He fought courageously against the oppression of England's king George. Allen's family, on the other hand, fought bravely beside William Wallace, the great Scottish hero who tried to free Scotland from the grips of English control. We were not going to give up our home without a fight. Fighting for what is right is in our DNA.

Christopher, the legal intern, arrived in time to join Allen and me in battle. We entered the room, and there sat the foreclosure mediator Ann

Mannen and Brian Bly. I noticed immediately she wasn't sitting anywhere near him. She had positioned herself between the parties. The conference began with Ms. Mannen addressing us in an upbeat tone regarding the successes she had with foreclosure meditation in saving people's home from sheriff's sale. She tossed a particularly prickly glance toward Brian when she said this. It was now his turn to make his case. We knew he could not be trusted based on his words in the waiting room minutes prior, so we listened intently.

He went on and on about how his client had been harmed by us not making our house payments, forgetting that his client had not put up one nickel for our home loan. He pulled out a copy of our note, which was supposed to be the evidence of the debt.

Allen was sitting closest to Brian Bly, and the minute the document hit the table, Allen asked to see the note. My husband took off his glasses, set them aside, and held the note in his hands for closer inspection. I held my breath because this couldn't be good. Whenever Allen takes off his glasses to look at something closer, there is trouble afoot.

Brian Bly got huffy and defensive before Allen even said anything. Brian said, "Seems like you want to play hardball, Mr. Ray. We have plenty of money to draw this out for years if you want to play tough. How are your finances holding up?"

Allen's face got red, and he put his glasses back on. I took a really deep breath because I knew what was about to happen. As I have said, what I admire most about my husband is his determination and his intellect in battle. He doesn't get caught up in the emotions of a fight but uses his knowledge. He has told me hundreds of times, "Knowledge is not power. When to use knowledge is power, Terry."

Allen got up from the conference table. He looked Brian Bly right in the eyes and said, "You had better have the original ink-signed note if you think you are going to take my home! This note is a fraud, and I will not sit here and listen to your lies or your threats anymore! I am ready to go to trial with a judge and jury to decide the fate of my home!"

He left the room, and there I was, alone with Brian and the magistrate. It was my turn to pick up where Allen had left off. My mind went to a quote I had put in a prominent place in my home: "Rise up, rise up, until the lambs become like lions." This was my time to rise up.

Ann Mannen asked me one question: "Mrs. Ray, how do you know that this isn't the original note?"

I sat up straight, dug down deep, and answered her question. "I know this isn't the original because of my work as a title examiner for the past ten years. I have had the opportunity to record in the county recorder's offices hundreds of original notes and mortgages. What Mr. Bly has brought here today is not an original. It is a copy of my original note. The color of the paper on his note is not pristine and white as an original would be. His copy doesn't have the recorder's stamp on it. You can't feel the impression of my signature or my husband's on the back of the paper that only putting pen to paper makes. His copy of our note is a fraud."

She looked at me, amazed at what I had said. She asked Brian to see his copy of our note and began examining the document closely. The last thing she did was to turn it over and feel where our signatures were written. Her fingers moved smoothly over the back of the paper, back and forth, back and forth. I knew at that moment, my presentation had been successful.

Mediator Ann Mannen looked up at Brian Bly and boldly announced that the conference was over. I am sure that his words of "enjoying taking people's homes away from them" were still on her mind. On May 18, 2009, she filed her report into the docket. She was requiring that counsel for ███████████ return the mediation questionnaire and attach all originals, the note and mortgage, to the questionnaire by May 29, 2009.

"Failure of plaintiff to comply would result in the dismissal of the case," the docket read. In eleven days, we would know if we were going to trial on our foreclosure.

CHAPTER 11

We Win

THIS WAS A time of great suspense. To deal with the time and the unknown outcome, we researched even more. Since the bank was malevolent enough to bring a copy to a pretrial mediation to take our home, we had better be sure we could prove beyond a shadow of a doubt that any copy they brought the next time was a fraud. We went back to our roots, to our profession as title examiners. We decided to go to the Cuyahoga County Recorder's Office in downtown Cleveland to review the actual process of recording an original mortgage.

During the great securitization gold rush (might as well call it what it was, a gold rush for Wall Street mega banks), Allen remembered recording as many as fifty original mortgages in one day. That was hours and hours of time standing in line to get mortgages recorded. There was a filing supervisor there named Ron Mack who had always been so knowledgeable and helpful to Allen in those days. We decided to go see Ron and ask his help once again.

We found him on the second floor of the administration building and began a conversation about how original mortgages were filed in 2005. We explained how we were being sued for foreclosure and the lender brought a copy of our note to the pretrial hearing. He said he wasn't surprised that they only brought the note to the hearing. It wasn't recorded with the mortgage unless the title company absolutely insisted. "Only the original mortgage and any riders would have been recorded in this office. The way we would distinguish the original mortgage is by this sticker here in the upper corner of your ink-signed mortgage," he said.

Allen and I looked at each other and had the exact same epiphany at that moment. Something as simple as a sticker, which you could see, feel, and actually pull off the mortgage doc if you wanted, could prove the mortgage to be an authentic first copy, an original. However, the black ink signatures on the mortgage and note should be raised and easily felt by our fingertips. Finally, the Cuyahoga County Recorder's Office issued extra stickers to the people filing original mortgages and notes, so it is possible to place these extra stickers onto fake documents. This is information that we filed away for future reference as we did not trust ███████████.

In the meantime, we checked the docket daily for our case, looking for clues as to what was going to happen to us and our home. The deadline of May 29, 2009, came and went, and there was nothing in the docket. No trial date had been set. What was happening? We received a phone call from our legal counsel who said the bank's lawyers at Carlisle, McNellie, Rini, Kramer & Ulrich Co., LPA had asked for an extension of time. They had misplaced the origination file with the copies of our mortgage and note and needed more time to locate it. More time was needed?! The suspense was agonizing.

Circumstances beyond our control had brought us to this moment. This was not how we planned to spend our lives: battling a mega bank worth trillions of dollars. But this is where we were today. We stood up for ourselves and fought back every step of the way for over two years since the day of Allen's fateful truck accident. The journey had been filled with so many twists and turns, but we never looked back or doubted our decision to stand together and fight for our home. We did not know our destiny, but we were ready for whatever came our way.

On the morning of July 9, 2009, almost two years to the day of Allen's accident, he opened the case docket for our foreclosure. There in bold letters, as if it were a movie marquee, was a final entry in the docket: "SINCE PLAINTIFF HAS FAILED TO COMPLY WITH THE COURT'S ORDER OF 6-08-09, THE MOTION OF DEFENDANTS ALLEN G RAY AND TERRY A RAY TO DISMISS IS GRANTED. THE CASE IS DISMISSED WITHOUT PREJUDICE AT PLAINTIFF'S COSTS. COURT COST ASSESSED TO THE PLAINTIFF(S). CLTMP 07/06/2009 NOTICE ISSUED." (See Appendix E)

We had *won*! We had beaten the largest bank in the world worth $2.7 trillion. They had not provided the court with the original mortgage or note and therefore could not prove they had the legal capacity to take our home away from us. ███████████ had utterly failed because they underestimated two middle-class individuals with meager means, but who had the hearts of warriors.

The laws that have governed property transfer for four hundred years in this country had been followed to the letter. We were entitled to sanctions and money damages, but we did not ask for them. This fight was not about money. This was about a journey of discovery and revelation. We learned about ourselves and each other and our tenacity to deal with whatever life tossed at us. The bank did not appeal the court's ruling either. It was a clean win.

Allen flew out of his home office and had the docket copy in his hand. "We won, Ter, we won!" he yelled.

I was stunned and started to cry. He gave me a high five and then a big hug.

With tears on my cheeks, I looked at him and felt such a sense of gratefulness and relief. He had survived a horrible truck crash and lived to see this successful day. We would not be leaving our home. Not on this day.

APPENDICES

Appendix A. Ray's Securitization Flow Chart

Appendix B. Who Really Gets a Free House?

Appendix C. DOCX Price List for Recreating Missing Documents

Appendix D. Wells Fargo vs. Jordan

Appendix E. ██████████████ vs. Ray

APPENDIX A

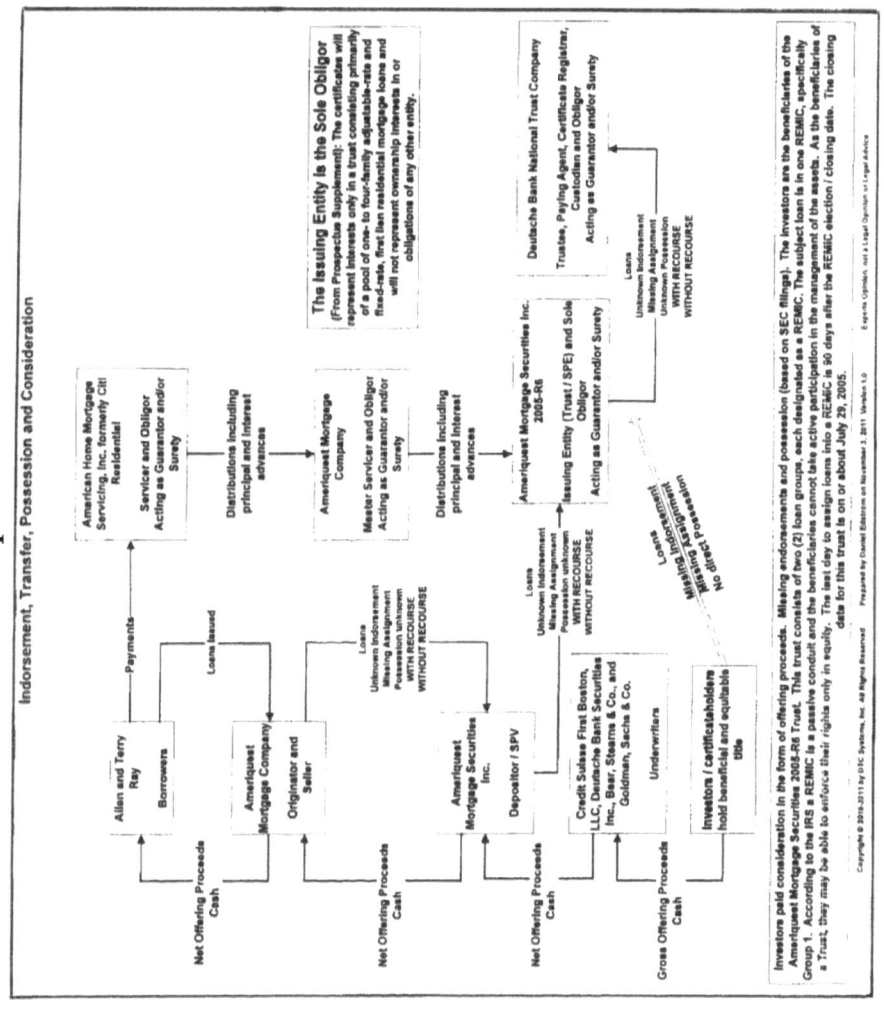

Ameriquest 2005-R6

Indorsement, Transfer, Possession and Consideration

WHO REALLY GETS A FREE HOUSE?

302 Westbridge Drive
Berea, Ohio 44017

America's Wholesale Lender

Description of Expense	Amount	The Rays' Contribution	▬▬▬▬ Contribution
Purchase Amount	$172,500	Property	0
Down Payment	$35,000	$35,000	0
Closing Costs	$7000	$7000	0
House Payments	$25,958	$25,958	0
Improvements	$30,000	$30,000	0
Insurance	$1630	$1630	0
Taxes	$9790	$9790	0

AmeriQuest Mortgage Company

Description of Expense	Amount	The Rays' Contribution	▬▬▬▬ Contribution
Re-Finance Amount	$201,000	Property	0
Closing Costs	$11,600	$11,600	0
House Payments	$51,220	$51,220	0
Improvements	$20,000	$20,000	0
Insurance	$4000	$4000	0
Taxes	$24,310	$24,310	0
Total Paid Out		$220,410	0

APPENDIX C

DOCX Home
About DOCX
What's Up @ DOCX
Contact DOCX

Online Services | Downloads | Services | Products

 *GETNET™ DOCUMENT RECOVERY*

DOCX's GetNet™ Document Recovery solution is a national network of runners that is engaged to provide document recovery, expedited recordation services, title searches, and insurance submissions.

The service is unique in that our clients can request that DOCX obtain any missing recordable documents through this web site through our online GetNet™ Work Order Form. Status of existing projects can also be obtained through our Online Services. We also accept work orders the "old fashioned" way via fax or mail. Upon receipt of the work order, DOCX will access the national network of runners, place the order and follow up to ensure prompt delivery.

GetNet™ was designed to assist mortgage servicers in meeting agency certifications and to avoid costly penalties for filing late satisfaction pieces.

GetNet™ Features

- A National Network of title runners retains presence in every county jurisdiction nationwide.
- Obtains missing mortgage documents, assignments, title policies and LGC/MICs.
- Expedites recordation by physically walking documents in to county recorder offices.

- Provides title searches to identify mortgage holders.
- Provides online reporting capabilities.

GETNET™ RATE SHEET

XCODE	SERVICE	AMOUNT
INF1	Obtain PIN Number from Online Public Records	$5.50 + SH
INF2	Obtain from Online Public Records Lot Block or Section	$5.50 + SH
INF3	Obtain Property Address	$5.50 + SH
INF4	Obtain Recorded Mortgage, Book, Page or Instrument Number	$12.95 + TPC
INF5	Obtain Vehicle Identification Number	$12.95 + SH
CT01	Cursory Title Search to Identify Mortgagee of Record	$15.95 + TPC
TS01	Perform Complete Title Search	$15.95 + TPC
SI01	Obtain Copy of Mortgage	$12.95 + TPC
SI02	Cure Defective Mortgage	$12.95 + TPC
SI03	Retrieve Certified Copies of Mortgages	$12.95 + TPC
PA01	Obtain Copy of Power of Attorney or Name Certification	$12.95 + TPC
PA02	Record Power of Attorney	$12.95 + TPC
PA03	Obtain Clerk Certified Copy of Power of Attorney	$12.95 + TPC
IC01	Obtain Copy of Installment Contract from VA	$15.95 + SH
SA01	Obtain Copy of Subordination Agreement	$15.95 + TPC
MA02	Obtain Copy of Modification	$15.95 + TPC
MI01	Obtain Copy of MIC	$12.95 + SH
MI02	Correct MIC	$12.95 + SH
LG01	Obtain Copy of LGC	$12.95 + SH
LG02	Correct LGC	$12.95 + SH

TP01	Obtain Copy of Title Policy Within 7 years (based on calender year)	$19.95 + TPC
TP02	Correct Existing Title Policy	$19.95 + TPC
TP03	Obtain Copy of Title Policy over 7 years (based on calendar year)	$29.95 + TPC
TP04	Obtain Quotes to Write and Order New Lenders Title Policy	$29.95 + TPC
TP05	Obtain Abstract from Title Company (State of Iowa)	$15.95 + TPC
TE02	Correct Title Policy Endorsement	$15.95 + TPC
LN02	Create Lost Note Affidavit	$12.95 + SH
NA01	Create Note Allonge	$12.95 + SH
NC01	Name Affidavit	$12.95 + SH
IA01	Obtain Copy of Assignment	$15.95 + TPC
IA02	Retrieve Certified Copies of Assignments	$15.95 + TPC
IA03	Create Missing Intervening Assignment	$35.00 + TPC
IA04	Record Prepared Assignments	$12.95 + TPC
IA05	Cure Defective Assignment	$12.95 + TPC
IS01	FHA and VA Mortgage Insurance Submission	$95.00 + TPC
UC01	Retrieving a UCC Package	$15.95 + TPC
CF01	Recreate Entire Collateral File	$95.00 + TPC
ER01	Expedited Recordation: Hand Carry Recordable Documents	$25.00 + TPC

Contact DOCX for volume discounts on orders of 200 items or more.

TPC = Third Party Costs include Title Runner, County Jurisdictional, courier and postage costs.

SH = Shipping costs.

The DOCX Service Fee will be invoiced upon receipt of the work order.

The Supreme Court of Ohio

Wells Fargo Bank, N.A.

v.

Oties Jordan et al.

Case No. 2009-1030

E N T R Y

Upon consideration of the jurisdictional memoranda filed in this case, the Court declines jurisdiction to hear the case.

(Cuyahoga County Court of Appeals; No. 91675)

THOMAS J. MOYER
Chief Justice

[Cite as *Wells Fargo Bank, N.A. v. Jordan*, 2009-Ohio-1092.]

Court of Appeals of Ohio

EIGHTH APPELLATE DISTRICT
COUNTY OF CUYAHOGA

JOURNAL ENTRY AND OPINION
No. 91675

WELLS FARGO BANK, N.A.

PLAINTIFF-APPELLEE

vs.

OTIES JORDAN, ET AL.

DEFENDANTS-APPELLANTS

JUDGMENT:
REVERSED AND REMANDED

Civil Appeal from the
Cuyahoga County Court of Common Pleas
Case No. CV-631753

BEFORE: Celebrezze, J., Rocco, P.J., and Kilbane, J.

RELEASED: March 12, 2009

JOURNALIZED:

FOR APPELLANTS

Oties Jordan (pro se)
Sylvia Jordan (pro se)
960 East 78th Street
Cleveland, Ohio 44103

ATTORNEY FOR APPELLEE

Benjamin D. Carnahan
Shapiro, Van Ess, Phillips & Barragate, L.L.P.
1500 West Third Street
Suite 455
Cleveland, Ohio 44113

N.B. This entry is an announcement of the court's decision. See App.R. 22(B) and 26(A); Loc.App.R. 22. This decision will be journalized and will become the judgment and order of the court pursuant to App.R. 22(C) unless a motion for reconsideration with supporting brief, per App.R. 26(A), is filed within ten (10) days of the announcement of the court's decision. The time period for review by the Supreme Court of Ohio shall begin to run upon the journalization of this court's announcement of decision by the clerk per App.R. 22(C). See, also, S.Ct. Prac.R. II, Section 2(A)(1).

FRANK D. CELEBREZZE JR., J.:

{¶1} Appellants, Oties Jordan, Sylvia Jordan, and Stay Focused, L.L.C., a company for which Oties Jordan is the statutory agent (collectively referred to as "Jordan"), bring this appeal challenging the trial court's entry of summary judgment in favor of appellee, Wells Fargo Bank ("WFB").

{¶2} On January 15, 2009, WFB filed a motion to dismiss for lack of a final appealable order. After a thorough review of the record, and for the reasons set forth below, we deny WFB's motion to dismiss and hold that the trial court erred by granting summary judgment.

{¶3} On January 3, 2003, Jordan executed a note and mortgage ("the Mortgage") with Delta Funding Corporation for property located on Wade Park Avenue in Cleveland, Ohio ("the Property"). On or about March 1, 2007, Jordan defaulted on the loan. On August 3, 2007, WFB filed a complaint against Jordan for money judgment, foreclosure, and relief. Attached to the complaint was a copy of the note and mortgage naming Delta Funding Corporation as the holder of the Mortgage. On November 8, 2007, Jordan filed his answer and counterclaim against WFB for fraud, negligence, and violations of federal and state creditor lending laws.

{¶4} On February 26, 2008, WFB filed a motion for summary judgment and a motion to dismiss Jordan's counterclaim. Despite extensions of time granted by the magistrate assigned to hear the case, Jordan did not file a timely opposition to WFB's motions. On April 7, 2008, the magistrate issued the following order: "As Plaintiff's motion to dismiss counterclaim presents matters outside the pleadings, said motion is deemed part of plaintiff's motion for summary judgment. Therefore, inasmuch as reasonable minds could conclude from the evidence submitted only that plaintiff is entitled to judgment and a decree of foreclosure, plaintiff's motion for summary judgment is granted. ***." Jordan filed objections to the magistrate's order.

{¶5} In its May 21, 2008 judgment entry, the trial court adopted the magistrate's decision in an entry that read: "The objection to the Magistrate's Decision is overruled. The Court adopts the Magistrate's Decision attached hereto and incorporated herein. Judgment for the substitute plaintiff against Oties Jordan, a.k.a. Oties Jordan Jr., in the sum of $72,690.93 with interest thereon at the rate of 9.24 [percent] per annum from March 1, 2007. Decree of foreclosure for substitute plaintiff. Pursuant to Civ.R. 54(B) the court finds no just cause for delay."

Final Appealable Order

{¶6} In its motion to dismiss, WFB argues that the trial court's entry is not a final appealable order because it does not set forth its own judgment. We disagree.

{¶7} Pursuant to Section 3(B)(2), Article IV of the Ohio Constitution, this court's appellate jurisdiction is limited to the review of final orders of lower courts. A trial court's order is final and appealable only if it meets the requirements of R.C. 2505.02 and, if applicable, Civ.R. 54(B). *In re Adoption of M.P.*, Franklin App. No. 07AP-278, 2007-Ohio-5660, ¶15, citing *Denham v. City of New Carlisle*, 86 Ohio St.3d 594, 596, 1999-Ohio-128, 716 N.E.2d 184.

{¶8} R.C. 2505.02(B) defines a final order, in pertinent part, as follows: "An order is a final order that may be reviewed, affirmed, modified, or reversed, with or without retrial, when it is one of the following: (1) An order that affects a substantial right in an action that in effect determines the action and prevents a judgment[.]"

{¶9} "For an order to determine the action and prevent a judgment for the party appealing, it must dispose of the whole merits of the cause or some separate and distinct branch thereof and leave nothing for the determination of the court." *Natl. City Commer. Capital Corp. v. AAAA at Your Serv. Inc.*, 114 Ohio St.3d 82, 2007-Ohio-2942, 868 N.E.2d 663.

{¶10} WFB takes issue here with whether the trial court's entry adopting the magistrate's decision is a final appealable order. "Civ.R. 53(E)(5) contains the following instruction: The court shall enter its own judgment on the issues submitted for action and report by the referee. Incorporating the referee's report without separately stating its own judgment does not constitute a final appealable order." *In re Michael* (1991), 71 Ohio App.3d 727, 595 N.E.2d 397. A trial court order stating merely that it is adopting a magistrate's decision is not a final appealable order. *Harkai v. Scherba Indus.* (2000), 136 Ohio App.3d 211, 736 N.E.2d 101. To constitute a final appealable order, a court's entry reflecting action on a magistrate's decision must be a separate and distinct instrument from the decision and must grant relief on the issues originally submitted to the court. *In re Jesmone Dortch* (1999), 135 Ohio App.3d 430, 734 N.E.2d 434.

{¶11} "[T]he trial court must*** enter its own independent judgment disposing of the matters at issue between the parties, such that the parties need not resort to any other document to ascertain the extent to which their rights and obligations have been determined. In other words, the judgment entry must be worded in such a manner that the parties can readily determine what is necessary to comply with the order of the court." *Burns v. Morgan*, 165 Ohio App.3d 694, 2006-Ohio-1213, 847 N.E.2d 1288, quoting *Yahraus v. City of Circleville*, 4th Dist. No. 00CA04, 2000-Ohio-2019, quoting *Lavelle v. Cox* (Mar. 15, 1991), 11th Dist. No. 90-T-4396.

{¶12} We find that the trial court's entry in this case is a final appealable order. In light of the fact that the magistrate incorporated WFB's motion to dismiss Jordan's counterclaim into its summary judgment motion, the judgment entry sets forth its judgment and a judgment amount in favor of WFB. Furthermore, the trial court order included the requisite Civ.R. 54(B) language, which grants this court jurisdiction to hear the appeal. WFB's motion to dismiss is denied.

Review and Analysis

{¶13} We next address the merits of Jordan's appeal, in which he raises three assignments of error for our review. We find Jordan's first assignment of error dispositive of the case.

{¶14} "I. The trial court erred in granting summary judgment to the substitute party plaintiff as genuine issues of material fact remained outstanding to be determined."

{¶15} In his first assignment of error, Jordan argues that summary judgment is improper because there was no evidence presented that WFB owned the Mortgage. Although we disagree with Jordan's claim that summary judgment was improper due to a lack of ownership evidence, we find that WFB did not have standing when it filed the complaint; therefore, the trial court erred by granting summary judgment in favor of WFB and should have dismissed this case without prejudice.

{¶16} "Civ.R. 56(C) specifically provides that before summary judgment may be granted, it must be determined that: (1) No genuine issue as to any material fact remains to be litigated; (2) the moving party is entitled to judgment as a matter of law; and (3) it appears from the evidence that reasonable minds can come to but one conclusion, and viewing such evidence most strongly in favor of the party against whom the motion for summary judgment is made, that conclusion is adverse to that party." *Temple v. Wean United Inc.* (1977), 50 Ohio St.2d 317, 327, 364 N.E.2d 267.

{¶17} It is well established that the party seeking summary judgment bears the burden of demonstrating that no issues of material fact exist for trial. *Celotex Corp. v. Catrett* (1986), 477 U.S. 317, 330, 106 S.Ct. 2548, 91 L.Ed.2d 265; *Mitseff v. Wheeler* (1988), 38 Ohio St.3d 112, 115, 526 N.E.2d 798. Doubts must be resolved in favor of the nonmoving party. *Murphy v. Reynoldsburg*, 65 Ohio St.3d 356, 1992-Ohio-95, 604 N.E.2d 138.

{¶18} In *Dresher v. Burt,* 75 Ohio St.3d 280, 1996-Ohio-107, 662 N.E.2d 264, the Ohio Supreme Court clarified the summary judgment standard as applied in *Wing v. Anchor Media Ltd.* (1991), 59 Ohio St.3d 108, 570 N.E.2d 1095. Under *Dresher*, "the moving party bears the initial responsibility of informing the trial court of the basis for the motion, *and identifying those portions of the record which demonstrate the absence of a genuine issue of fact or material element of the nonmoving party's claim.*" Id. at 296. (Emphasis in original.) The nonmoving party has a reciprocal burden of specificity and cannot rest on mere allegations or denials in the pleadings. Id. at 293. The nonmoving party must set forth "specific facts" by the means listed in Civ.R. 56(C) showing that a genuine issue for trial exists. Id.

{¶19} This court reviews the lower court's granting of summary judgment de novo. *Brown v. County Commrs.* (1993), 87 Ohio App.3d 704, 622 N.E.2d 1153. An appellate court reviewing the grant of summary judgment must follow the standards set forth in Civ.R. 56(C). "The reviewing court evaluates the record □ □ □ in a light most favorable to the nonmoving party □ □ □ . [T]he motion must be overruled if reasonable minds could find for the party opposing the motion." *Saunders v. McFaul* (1990), 71 Ohio App.3d 46, 50, 593 N.E.2d 24; *Link v. Leadworks Corp.* (1992), 79 Ohio App.3d 735, 741, 607 N.E.2d 1140.

{¶20} Civ.R. 17(A) states that "[e]very action shall be prosecuted in the name of the real party in interest. □ □ □ No action shall be dismissed on the ground that it is not prosecuted in the name of the real party in interest until a reasonable time has been allowed after objection for ratification of commencement of the action by, or joinder or substitution of, the real party in interest. Such ratification, joinder, or substitution shall have the same effect as if the action had been commenced in the name of the real party in interest."

{¶21} "A party lacks standing to invoke the jurisdiction of a court unless he has, in an individual or a representative capacity, some real interest in the subject matter of the action. *State ex rel. Dallman v. Court of Common Pleas* (1973), 35 Ohio St.2d 176, 298 N.E.2d 515, syllabus. The Eleventh Appellate District has held that 'Civ.R. 17 is not applicable when the plaintiff is not the proper party to bring the case and, thus, does not have standing to do so. A person lacking any right or interest to protect may not invoke the jurisdiction of a court.' *Northland Ins. Co. v. Illuminating Co.*, 11th Dist. Nos. 2002-A-0058 and 2002-A-0066, 2004-Ohio-1529, at ¶17 (internal quotations and citations omitted). The court also noted that 'Civ.R. 17(A) was not applicable unless the plaintiff had standing to invoke the jurisdiction of the court in the first place, either in an individual or representative capacity, with some real interest in the subject matter. Civ.R. 17 only applies if the action is commenced by one who is sui juris or the proper party to bring the action.' *Travelers Indemn. Co. v. R. L. Smith Co.* (Apr. 13, 2001), 11th Dist. No. 2000-L-014." *Wells Fargo Bank, N.A. v. Byrd*, 178 Ohio App.3d 285, 2008-Ohio-4603, 897 N.E.2d 722.

{¶22} The holder of rights or interest in property is a necessary party to a foreclosure action. See *Hembree v. Mid-America Fed. Sav. & Loan Assn.* (1989), 64 Ohio App.3d 144, 152, 580 N.E.2d 1103.

{¶23} In ▇▇▇▇▇▇ *National Trust Co. v. Steele* (6th Cir., Jan. 8, 2008), Case No. 2:07-CV-886, the court held: "While a court has no duty to search the record and may properly limit its review of an unopposed motion for summary judgment to the facts relied on by defendant, *Guarino v. Brookfield Township Trustees,* 980 F.2d 399, 404-05 and 407 (6th Cir. 1992), it cannot enter judgment if the moving party is not entitled to judgment as a matter of law. Rule 56(c), Fed.R.Civ.P. Several judges have held that a complaint must be dismissed if the plaintiff cannot prove that it owned the note and mortgage on the date the complaint was filed. E.g., *In re Foreclosure Cases,* (N.D. Ohio 2007), Case Nos. 1:07CV2282, et seq., (Boyko, J.); *In re Foreclosure Cases* (S.D. Ohio 2007), 521 F. Supp.2d 650, (Rose, J.). Thus, if plaintiff has offered no evidence that it owned the note and mortgage when the complaint was filed, it would not be entitled to judgment as a matter of law."

{¶24} In *Wells Fargo Bank, N.A. v. Byrd,* supra, where Wells Fargo filed suit on its own behalf but acquired the mortgage from the original lender after filing, the court held that, "in a foreclosure action, a bank that was not the mortgagee when suit was filed cannot cure its lack of standing by subsequently obtaining an interest in the mortgage."

{¶25} Our facts are exactly the same here. Delta Funding Corporation owned the Mortgage for the Property on August 3, 2007, the date WFB filed its complaint against Jordan. On September 24, 2007, WFB filed a Notice of Filing of Final Judicial Report. Attached to the Notice were a Final Judicial Report and an Assignment of Mortgage, indicating the Mortgage had been assigned to WFB on August 22, 2007, nearly three weeks after it filed its complaint. In short, WFB was not the real party in interest on the date it filed its complaint seeking foreclosure against Jordan.

{¶26} Thus, WFB lacked standing to bring a foreclosure action against Jordan. As such, the trial court erred in granting summary judgment in favor of WFB because WFB was not entitled to judgment as a matter of law. We sustain Jordan's first assignment of error, reverse summary judgment, and order the trial court to dismiss the complaint without prejudice.

{¶27} Having sustained Jordan's first assignment of error, we find his remaining assignments of error are moot.[11]

{¶28} This cause is reversed and remanded to the lower court for further proceedings consistent with this opinion.

It is ordered that appellants recover of said appellee costs herein taxed.

The Court finds there were reasonable grounds for this appeal.

It is ordered that a special mandate issue out of this court directing the common pleas court to carry this judgment into execution.

A certified copy of this entry shall constitute the mandate pursuant to Rule 27 of the Rules of Appellate Procedure.

FRANK D. CELEBREZZE JR., JUDGE

KENNETH A. ROCCO, P.J., and
MARY EILEEN KILBANE, J., CONCUR

APPENDIX

Appellant's remaining Assignments of Error:

II.   That the trial court erred in granting the motion of Wells Fargo Bank to substitute party plaintiff filed 11/16/07 on 11/21/07 without hearing, substantial basis therefore, or even providing the defendant with an opportunity to receive, review or reply to the motion.

III.   That the trial court erred in determining it had jurisdiction to proceed in this foreclosure contrary to the Federal Court determinations and the standard within the Court of Common Pleas Cuyahoga County.

---

[1]   Appellant's remaining Assignments of Error are included in the Appendix to this Opinion.

APPENDIX E

58329939

IN THE COURT OF COMMON PLEAS
CUYAHOGA COUNTY, OHIO

███████████████████

Plaintiff

ALLEN G. RAY ETAL

Defendant

Case No: CV-████████

Judge: TIMOTHY J MCGINTY

JOURNAL ENTRY

87 DIS. W/O PREJ-FINAL

SINCE PLAINTIFF HAS FAILED TO COMPLY WITH THE COURT'S ORDER OF 6-08-09. THE MOTION OF DEFENDANTS ALLEN G RAY AND TERRY A RAY TO DISMISS IS GRANTED. THE CASE IS DISMISSED WITHOUT PREJUDICE AT PLAINTIFF'S COSTS.
  COURT COST ASSESSED TO THE PLAINTIFF(S).

T. J. McGinty

Judge Signature   07/09/2009
                                   CPSB1

Case Number: CV-███████████

Case Title: ████████████████████ vs. ALLEN G. RAY ETAL

Image Viewer: AlternaTIFF

DOCKET INFORMATION

Date	Side	Type	Description	Image
09/11/2009	P1	CS	REFUND CASE COST DEPOSIT TO CARLISLE MCNELLIE RINI KRAMER & ULRICH	
07/09/2009	N/A	JE	SINCE PLAINTIFF HAS FAILED TO COMPLY WITH THE COURT'S ORDER OF 6-08-09. THE MOTION OF DEFENDANTS ALLEN G RAY AND TERRY A RAY TO DISMISS IS GRANTED. THE CASE IS DISMISSED WITHOUT PREJUDICE AT PLAINTIFF'S COSTS. COURT COST ASSESSED TO THE PLAINTIFF(S). CLTMP 07/06/2009 NOTICE ISSUED	▤
06/25/2009	D	MO	DEFENDANT(S) ALLEN G RAY(D1) and TERRY A RAY(D2) MOTION TO DISMISS. MATTHEW G BRUCE 0083769 07/09/2009—GRANTED	
06/08/2009	N/A	JE	PLAINTIFF'S MOTION FOR EXTENSION OF TIME TO FILE LENDER'S QUESTIONNAIRE IS GRANTED. PLAINTIFF MAY FILE ITS COMPLETED LENDER'S QUESTIONNAIRE ON OR BEFORE 6-12-09. FAILURE TO DO SO WILL RESULT IN DISMISSAL OF PLAINTIFF'S COMPLAINT WITHOUT PREJUDICE. CLTMP 06/05/2009 NOTICE ISSUED	▤
05/29/2009	P1	MO	P1 ████████████████████ ██████████████ MOTION FOR EXTENSION OF TIME TO FILE LENDER'S QUESTIONNAIRE. JAMES L SASSANO 0062253 06/08/2009—GRANTED	

TERRY PUFFER RAY & ALLEN RAY

05/22/2009   N/A   MG   CASE MGMNT CONFERENCE SET FOR
09/11/2009 AT 09:00 AM. FAILURE TO
APPEAR MAY RESULT IN DISMISSAL OF
AFFIRMATIVE CLAIMS FOR RELIEF. IF A
PARTY SEEKING JUDGMENT HAS FILED
A MOTION FOR DEFAULT JUDGMENT
AT LEAST 14 DAYS BEFORE THE DATE
OF THE CMC, THE CMC WILL ALSO
BE A HEARING ON THE MOTION FOR
DEFAULT JUDGMENT. ANY CLAIMANT
WISHING TO PROCEED ON HIS CLAIMS
MUST TAKE AFFIRMATIVE STEPS TO
PROSECUTE HIS CLAIMS BEFORE THE
CASE MANAGEMENT CONFERENCE.
FAILURE TO DO SO WILL RESULT
IN DISMISSAL OF THE CASE. CLTMP
05/21/2009 NOTICE ISSUED

05/21/2009   N/A   SC   CASE MGMNT CONFERENCE
SCHEDULED FOR 05/29/2009 AT 09:30 AM
IS CANCELLED.

05/18/2009   N/A   JE   PRE-MEDIATION CONFERENCE HELD.
THE PARTIES MUST COMPLETE THE
PROPERTY OWNER'S MEDIATION
QUESTIONNAIRE OR THE RETURN
THEM AND ALL DOCUMENTS REQUIRED
THEREIN ON OR BEFORE 05/29/2009 TO
THE MEDIATOR AT THE FOLLOWING
ADDRESS: ADR DEPARTMENT, JUSTICE
CENTER—4TH FLOOR, 1200 ONTARIO
STREET, CLEVELAND, OHIO 44113. FAILURE
OF PLAINTIFF TO COMPLY WILL RESULT
IN DISMISSAL OF THE CASE. FAILURE OF
THE PROPERTY OWNER TO COMPLY WILL
RESULT IN THE RETURN OF THE CASE
TO THE FORECLOSURE MAGISTRATE
FOR FURTHER PROCEEDINGS. CLTMP
05/15/2009 NOTICE ISSUED

04/09/2009   N/A   JE   PRE MEDIATION CONFERENCE SET FOR 05/15/2009 AT 03:00 PM. FAILURE OF THE PROPERTY OWNER, OR PROPERTY OWNER'S COUNSEL, TO APPEAR IN PERSON AT THE PRE-MEDIATION CONFERENCE WILL RESULT THE CASE BEING RETURNED TO THE FORECLOSURE DOCKET. FAILURE OF THE LENDER'S COUNSEL TO APPEAR IN PERSON AT THE PRE-MEDIATION CONFERENCE WILL RESULT IN DISMISSAL OF THE LENDER'S CLAIMS WITHOUT PREJUDICE. PLEASE REPORT TO THE ALTERNATIVE DISPUTE RESOLUTION (ADR) DEPARTMENT ON THE 4TH FLOOR OF THE JUSTICE CENTER, 1200 ONTARIO, CLEVELAND, OHIO, FOR THE PRE-MEDIATION CONFERENCE. CLTMP 04/08/2009 NOTICE ISSUED

03/18/2009   N/A   MG   CASE MGMNT CONFERENCE SET FOR 05/29/2009 AT 09:30 AM. FAILURE TO APPEAR MAY RESULT IN DISMISSAL OF AFFIRMATIVE CLAIMS FOR RELIEF. CLTMP 03/17/2009 NOTICE ISSUED

03/17/2009   N/A   SC   CASE MGMNT CONFERENCE SCHEDULED FOR 04/07/2009 AT 01:30 PM IS CANCELLED.

01/16/2009   N/A   MG   CASE MGMNT CONFERENCE SET FOR 04/07/2009 AT 01:30 PM. FAILURE TO APPEAR MAY RESULT IN DISMISSAL OF AFFIRMATIVE CLAIMS FOR RELIEF. CLTMP 01/15/2009 NOTICE ISSUED

01/15/2009   N/A   MG   CASE CALLED FOR DEFAULT HEARING. SINCE ALL DEFENDANTS HAVE ANSWERED PLAINTIFF'S COMPLAINT, PLAINTIFF'S MOTION FOR DEFAULT JUDGMENT IS DENIED. THE CASE WILL BE REFERRED TO THE FORECLOSURE MEDIATION PROGRAM FOR EVALUATION BY SEPARATE ORDER. CLTMP 01/14/2009 NOTICE ISSUED

01/15/2009   N/A   MG   THE MAGISTRATE HAS DETERMINED THAT THE CASE MAY BE SUITABLE FOR MEDIATION. THE CASE IS REFERRED TO THE COURT'S FORECLOSURE MEDIATION PROGRAM FOR FURTHER EVALUATION. ALL DISCOVERY AND MOTION PRACTICE IS STAYED PENDING THE MEDIATOR'S FINAL DETERMINATION OF SUITABILITY OF THE CASE FOR MEDIATION. CLTMP 01/14/2009 NOTICE ISSUED

01/13/2009   N/A   AF   AFFIDAVIT AS TO INTEREST RATE . . . . (W) . . . .

12/31/2008   P1   OT   P1 ███████████████████████ ████████ REPLY TO DEFENDANT'S COUNTERCLAIM . . . . W . . . . JAMES L SASSANO 0062253

12/31/2008   P1   OT   P1 ███████████████████████ ████████ NOTICE OF DEFAULT HEARING . . . . W . . . . JANUARY 14TH 2009 @ 2:00PM . . . . JAMES L SASSANO 0062253

12/15/2008   N/A   MG   MOTION FOR DEFAULT JUDGMENT IS SET FOR HEARING ON 01/14/2009 AT 02:00PM BEFORE MAGISTRATE STEPHEN M BUCHA, 310 W. LAKESIDE, 7TH FL. THE MOVING PARTY MUST SEND NOTICE OF THE DATE AND TIME OF THIS HEARING AND A COPY OF THE MOTION TO ALL PARTIES, INCLUDING THOSE WHO HAVE YET TO ENTER AN APPEARANCE. AT LEAST 14 DAYS IN ADVANCE OF THE HEARING. FAILURE TO APPEAR MAY RESULT IN DISMISSAL OF THE CLAIMS OR AN ENTRY OF JUDGMENT. CLTMP 12/12/2008 NOTICE ISSUED

12/04/2008   D1   AN   DEFENDANT(S) ALLEN G RAY(D1) and TERRY A RAY(D2) ANSWER AND COUNTERCLAIM. JOHN C OBERHOLTZER 0021578

12/03/2008	P1	MO	P1 ███████████████ ███████ MOTION FOR DEFAULT JUDGMENT . . . . (W) . . . . JAMES L SASSANO 0062253 01/15/2009—DENIED
12/03/2008	N/A	OT	FINAL JUDICIAL REPORT . . . . (W) . . . .
12/03/2008	N/A	AF	MILITARY AFFIDAVIT . . . . (W) . . . .
11/12/2008	D2	SR	12820504 ON 11/05/2008 I SERVED THE WITHIN NAMED RAY/TERRY/A BY SERVING A TRUE AND CERTIFIED COPY THEREOF WITH ALL THE ENDORSEMENTS THEREON. S.P.S.
11/12/2008	D1	SR	12820503 ON 11/05/2008 I SERVED THE WITHIN NAMED RAY/ALLEN/G BY SERVING A TRUE AND CERTIFIED COPY THEREOF WITH ALL THE ENDORSEMENTS THEREON. S.P.S.
11/07/2008	D1	SR	CERTIFIED MAIL RECEIPT NO. 12820500 RETURNED BY U.S. MAIL DEPARTMENT 11/07/2008 RAY/ALLEN/G MAIL RECEIVED AT ADDRESS 11/06/2008 SIGNED BY OTHER.
11/07/2008	D2	SR	CERTIFIED MAIL RECEIPT NO. 12820501 RETURNED BY U.S. MAIL DEPARTMENT 11/07/2008 RAY/TERRY/A MAIL RECEIVED BY ADDRESSEE 11/06/2008.
11/06/2008	N/A	SF	MAGISTRATE STEPHEN M BUCHA ASSIGNED (MANUALLY)
11/06/2008	N/A	JE	IT IS ORDERED BY THE COURT THAT THIS CAUSE BE REFERRED TO THE COURT MAGISTRATE TO TRY THE ISSUES OF LAW AND FACT ARISING THEREIN AND REPORT WITHOUT UNNECESSARY DELAY. A PARTY SEEKING A DEFAULT JUDGMENT MUST FILE A MOTION FOR

TERRY PUFFER RAY & ALLEN RAY

11/05/2008	D2	SR	SUMS COMPLAINT(12820501) SENT BY CERTIFIED MAIL TO: TERRY A RAY 302 WEST BRIDGE DRIVE BEREA, OH 44017-0000
11/05/2008	D1	SR	SUMS COMPLAINT(12820500) SENT BY CERTIFIED MAIL TO: ALLEN G RAY 302 WEST BRIDGE DRIVE BEREA, OH 44017-0000
11/04/2008	D2	SR	SUMS COMPLAINT (12820504) SENT BY SPECIAL PROCESS SERVER TO: TERRY A RAY 302 WEST BRIDGE DRIVE BEREA, OH 44017-0000
11/04/2008	D1	SR	SUMS COMPLAINT (12820503) SENT BY SPECIAL PROCESS SERVER TO: ALLEN G RAY 302 WEST BRIDGE DRIVE BEREA, OH 44017-0000
11/03/2008	P1	SR	PRELIMINARY JUDICIAL REPORT FILED.
11/03/2008	P1	SR	COMPLAINT FILED. SERVICE REQUEST—SUMMONS BY PROCESS SERVER AND CERTIFIED MAIL TO THE DEFENDANT(S).
11/03/2008	P1	SR	FIELD SERVICE REPRESENTATIVE OR OTHER CONTACT: NAME JAMES SASSANO NUMBER (216) 360-7200
11/03/2008	D2	CS	WRIT FEE
11/03/2008	D1	CS	WRIT FEE
11/03/2008	D2	CS	WRIT FEE
11/03/2008	D1	CS	WRIT FEE
11/03/2008	N/A	SF	JUDGE TIMOTHY J MCGINTY ASSIGNED (RANDOM)
11/03/2008	P1	SF	SPECIAL PROJECTS FUND FEE

11/03/2008	P1	SF	LEGAL RESEARCH
11/03/2008	P1	SF	LEGAL NEWS
11/03/2008	P1	SF	LEGAL AID
11/03/2008	P1	SF	COMPUTER FEE
11/03/2008	P1	SF	CLERK'S FEE
11/03/2008	P1	SF	DEPOSIT AMOUNT PAID CARLISLE MCNELLIE RINI KRAMER & ULRICH
11/03/2008	P1	SF	DEPOSIT AMOUNT PAID CARLISLE MCNELLIE RINI KRAMER & ULRICH
11/03/2008	N/A	SF	CASE FILED

TERRY PUFFER RAY & ALLEN RAY

REFERENCES

Books

Cohan, William D. 2009. *House of Cards: A Tale of Hubris and Wretched Excess on Wall Street*. New York: Anchor.

Faber, David. 2009. *And Then the Roof Caved In: How Wall Street's Greed and Stupidity Brought Capitalism to Its Knees*. Hoboken: John Wiley & Sons.

Floyd, Charles F., and Allen T. Marcus. 2002. *Real Estate Principles*. 7th ed. Chicago: Dearborn Real Estate Education.

Harris, Jack C., and Jack P. Friedman. 2001. *Barron's Real Estate Handbook*. 5th ed. Hauppauge: Barron's Educational Series.

Martin, Iris. 2009. *Mortgage Wars: How You Can Fight Fraud and Reverse Foreclosure*. San Diego: Pacific Coast.

Taibbi, Matt. 2010. *Griftopia: Bubble Machines, Vampire Squids, and the Long Con That Is Breaking America*. New York: Spiegel & Grau.

Tett, Gillian. 2009. *Fool's Gold: The Inside Story of J.P. Morgan and How Wall St. Greed Corrupted Its Bold Dream and Created a Financial Catastrophe*. New York: Free Press.

Seminars

Charney, April. 2008. "Basic Foreclosure Litigation." Paper presented at a seminar at the Legal Advocacy Center of Central Florida, April 11.

Garfield, Neil. 2009. "The Garfield Continuum." Paper presented at the Foreclosure Defense Workshop, September 13.

Keiser, Brad, and Neil F. Garfield. 2010. "The Garfield Continuum." Paper presented at a seminar for Forensic Mortgage Analysis, March 20-24.

Websites

Epstein, Lisa. "Florida Foreclosure Issues." foreclosurehamlet.org.
Garfield, Neil F. "The Garfield Continuum." livinglies.wordpress.com.

Mortgage Electronic Registration Systems. merinc.org.

Mortgage Servicing Fraud. msfraud.org.

Redman, Michael. "Foreclosure Fraud Issues." 4closurefraud.wordpress.com.

Russell, Glenn F., Jr. "Massachusetts Foreclosure Defense." foreclosure sinmass.com.

Securities and Exchange Commission. sec.gov.

Szymoniak, Lynn. "Document and Robo-Signing Issues." frauddigest.com.

TERRY PUFFER RAY & ALLEN RAY

INDEX

F

Faber, David, 9
Federal Reserve, 16, 28
Fifth Third Bank, 23
final judicial report, 52, 90
Financial Services Modernization Act of 1999, 16, 28
foreclosure, 13, 17-18, 21-22, 32, 36, 38-39, 42-45, 47-48, 50, 52-54, 58-60, 90
foreclosure meditation, 57, 90
foreclosure prevention, 53, 90
401K, 29
Freilich, Felix, 20
Freilich, Max, 20

G

Garfield, Neal, 23-24, 29
Garfield, Neil, 34, 44
Germany, 20, 90
Gramm-Leach-Bliley Act. *See* Financial Services Modernization Act of 1999
Greenspan, Alan, 28

H

hedge fund, 24, 29-31, 90
home loan, 13, 21-22, 24, 36, 49, 57
home mortgages, 14, 16, 21, 28, 35, 90, 93
homeowner's policies, 24, 90
housing crisis, 17, 25, 90

I

insurance policies, 16, 24, 90
investment banks, 18, 24-25, 28-29, 31, 90
investors, 16, 21-23, 29-32, 34-35, 42, 90
IRS (Internal Revenue Service), 18

J

Jordan, Oties, 54-55
Jordan, Sylvia, 54-55
Justice Center, 55, 90

K

Kaiser, Brad, 23-24, 29
Kaptur, Marcy, 18

L

Lakewood, Ohio, 14-15
lender, 16, 22, 25, 33, 46-48, 50, 53, 59, 90
Living Lies (blog), 23
loan, securitized, 41
loan modification, 11-13, 42, 46-47, 52-54, 90, 93
Lou (craftsman), 15
lower court, 54, 90
Lumina Q, 34, 43

M

Mannen, Ann, 55-57
McGinty, Timothy J., 55
Medina, Ohio, 49

Toledo, Ohio, 9
True Temper, 20
trustee, 13, 16, 31, 34, 42-43, 91
trust fund, 31, 91
Truth in Lending Act, 25, 34

U

UL (Underwriters Laboratory), 16
underwriters, 31
United States, 10, 16, 18, 20, 35-36, 38-39, 92-93

V

Volvo Car Corporation, 20

W

Wallace, William, 56
Wall Street, 14, 16, 18, 21-25, 28-31, 33-38, 53, 59, 92
Wells Fargo Bank, 16, 54-55, 92
Wetherbee, Christopher L., 55
World War II, 27
Wright, Frank Lloyd, 11

TERRY PUFFER RAY & ALLEN RAY

T ERRY PUFFER RAY is the author of Failure to Comply: We Fought a Wallstreet Giant and Won. She brings over a decade of examining titles for one of the largest foreclosure law firms in the United States and the second largest title insurance company. Working alongside outstanding foreclosure attorneys, as well as lead counsel for a $15 billion dollar title company, Terry gained extensive knowledge of foreclosure proceedings, loan modification, title clearance, and securitization of home mortgages, as well as credit default swaps. As we know now, it was the massive amount of credit default swaps that contributed to the financial collapse of 2008.

Terry lives with her husband Allen and co-author in northeastern Ohio.

Allen Glenn Ray, co-author, is a 1965 graduate of Harbor High School. He later taught and coached for the Harbor Mariners during the 1970's when one of his track teams set the all-time record for Ashtabula County in the mile relay. After leaving the field of education, Mr. Ray worked as an Industrial manager in quality control, as a wedding photographer, as a research scientist in computer development, as a medical technologist for Innova Corporation, and finally as a title examiner/abstractor.

His diverse work history and research skills enable him to figure out how mortgage securitization destroyed his residential mortgage.

Mr. Ray has written two other works of non-fiction prior to Failure to Comply. In 1996 he wrote his master's thesis entitled The Relationship Between Injuries and Training of Master's Decathletes. In 2000, he wrote his doctoral dissertation entitled: A Historical Evaluation of Intelligence Testing in America: Advancement of the Parallel Distribution Processing Paradigm.

He retired in 2009 and now lives in northeastern Ohio with his wife and their six cats.

www.ingramcontent.com/pod-product-compliance
Lightning Source LLC
Chambersburg PA
CBHW022117170526
45157CB00004B/1675